baseball

A History of the National Pastime

MARK STEWART

FRANKLIN WATTS
A Division of Grolier Publishing
New York • London • Hong Kong • Sydney
Danbury, Connecticut

Cover design by Dave Klaboe   Series design by Molly Heron

Photographs ©: Archive Photos: 89; Brown Brothers: 6, 29, 50 bottom, 61, 69, 72, 75; John Klein: 97, 101, 104, 105, 111, 116 right, 117 118; National Baseball Hall Of Fame Library, Cooperstown, N.Y.: 8, 12, 18, 35, 38, 53, 55, 79, 81, 87, 88, 91, 93, 109; Paul Thompson: 42; Reuters/Archive Photos: 103 (Blaka Sell); Reuters/Corbis-Bettman: 114 (Joe Giza); Sports Photo Masters, Inc.: 119 (Jonathan Eric), 95, 102, 106, 107, 113, 116 left (Mitchell B. Reibel); Team Stewart, Inc.: 22, 50 top (Geo.Burke), 51, 73, 27 (F.H.F.), 32 (Fan Craze), 37, 40, 44, 57 (George Routledge and Sons), 59 (Gum, Inc.), 48 (Hal Lebowitz), 24 (Horton Publishing Co.), 58, 77 (MacFadden Publications), 67 left (Ron Lewis/Capital Cards), 67 right, 84 left, 92 (T.C.G.), 33 (TCMA, Ltd.), 54, 64, (The Baseball Magazine Co.); UPI/Corbis-Bettmann: 5, 30, 66, 71, 84 right, 86, 99, 108.

Visit Franklin Watts on the Internet at:

http://publishing.grolier.com

Library of Congress Cataloging-in-Publication Data

Stewart, Mark
    Baseball : a history of the national pastime / Mark Stewart.
    p. cm. — (The Watts history of sports)
    Includes bibliographical references and index.
    Summary: A comprehensive history of baseball focusing on its evolution, momentous events,
        and key personalities.
    ISBN 0-531-11455-4
    1. Baseball—United States—History—Juvenile literature. [1. Baseball—History.] I. Title II. Series.
    GV867.5.S84 1998
    796.357'0973—dc21   97-18066
                                        CIP
                                        AC

1 2 3 4 5 6 7 8 9 10 R 07 06 05 04 03 02 01 00 99 98

CONTENTS

THE HISTORY OF BASEBALL

A Mythical Beginning

Abner Doubleday did not invent baseball. For more than 90 years, this myth about the origin of the game has been drummed into the heads of millions of schoolchildren. And it's just plain wrong. Baseball developed slowly, changing with and reacting to the times and eventually coming to reflect the times. That's why the game is called America's national pastime. Baseball is no less important just because it did not spring from the mind of one American. In fact, one could easily argue that it is even more American. So why all the fuss about Doubleday?

It began in 1905, when a special commission was formed to investigate the beginnings of baseball. According to the findings of this group, an old man claiming to be one of Doubleday's childhood friends swore that he was present in 1839 in the village of Cooperstown, New York, when Abner "invented" baseball. Sometime later, an old, rotting baseball was found among Doubleday's personal effects. This was viewed as the proof the old man's story was true. Today, the very same ball is on display at the Baseball Hall of Fame in Cooperstown, and each summer a special Hall of Fame exhibition game is played on nearby Doubleday Field. For baseball to face up to the facts, at this point, would present a big problem, for there would be a lot of undoing to do.

The facts, however, clearly point to an alternate and much more reasonable account of how baseball developed in the

The New York Knickerbockers and the Brooklyn Excelsiors posed for this photograph before an 1858 game.

For many years Abner Doubleday, pictured here in his army uniform, was incorrectly called the "Inventor of Baseball."

United States. The facts also point away from Doubleday, who in 1839 would have been a cadet at the U.S. Military Academy in West Point, New York, when he supposedly invented the game. Cooperstown was a very long way from West Point, and Doubleday would have had no business being there. Also, found along with the famous ball were several diaries that chronicled his life in great detail from the 1830s right on through his distinguished career as an officer in the Mexican War and the Civil War—a span of more than a quarter-century. No mention of baseball was ever found in these writings, despite the fact that the game was immensely popular while Doubleday was alive. Would it be unreasonable to believe

that a person giving birth to the first great team sport played in the United States might take some credit for his invention?

Stool Ball, One-o-Cat, and Rounders

References to baseball, which was most often written as "base ball" during the 19th century, have been found as far back as the late-1700s, alongside references to other children's games. These games include bat and ball, stool ball, one-o-cat, and bat and ball. They all had in common one basic premise: a ball is tossed to a batter, the batter hits it with a club or stick, and then runs to one or more bases. The closest relative to the game we now call baseball was rounders, which came to the United States with English immigrants during the 18th century. Rounders featured four bases, a feeder, and a striker (pitcher and batter). Its rules stated a player could be put "out" by swinging and missing three times, being struck by a thrown ball, or when a batted ball was caught by a defensive player. It does not take an expert historian to see the obvious similarities between baseball and this game from England. Furthermore, almost every baseball-like game played during the first few decades of the 19th century had its roots in England.

America in the early part of the 19th century was a very different place than it is today. Obviously, there were far fewer people, living in far fewer cities and towns, and those cities and towns were far smaller than they would be just 50 years later. What was really different (especially for young people) was that the playing of sports was very much frowned upon at the time. Working up a good sweat was viewed as unhealthy.

Games that featured physical competition were almost unheard of. None of today's major team sports existed back then, and even simple competitions—such as running, jumping, throwing, and lifting—were viewed as pastimes for children and low-class ruffians.

It was not that Americans lacked the strength, drive, and cunning to participate in sports. On the contrary, these were the defining qualities of the nation as it expanded ever westward during the 1800s. There was simply a great resistance to any kind of adult play.

Part of the problem may have been the sports revolution that was taking place across the Atlantic Ocean. The English people were mad for outdoor games, particularly rugby, soccer, and cricket. In the early 19th century, Americans hated the English. There were still a few veterans of the Revolutionary War around, and thousands of veterans from the War of 1812, when the British had invaded the United States and burned the public buildings in Washington, D.C. In the northern states, especially, there was tremendous anti-British sentiment, for the English still had an economic foothold in the south, where they bought cotton, tobacco, and many of the raw materials needed to further expand their global empire. If Englishmen liked to play games, then Americans would not play at all.

Needless to say, this attitude did not fit the times very well. More and more people in the United States found themselves living in cities and working at jobs that did not require physical labor. They had a lot more time and energy on their hands than their rural counterparts. Not surprisingly, there was an ever-increasing demand for some sort of outlet; there was a real and growing need for some sort of organized sport for adults. The question was, what might be an appropriate sport?

The natural direction to turn was toward cricket, a game somewhat similar to baseball that involves throwing, hitting, running, and catching. On the surface, the game seemed ideal: it was challenging yet safe, it could be played at a civilized pace, there was plenty of strategy involved, and it had a long tradition as a game for grown-ups. There were, however, several problems with this choice. First of all, it took a very long time to play—sometimes more than a day. Second, it was a sport associated with the rich, which limited its appeal. And third, cricket was a game of British origin, which to many made it instantly unacceptable. Americans wanted a game they could call their own. They also wanted a game that would not be called childish.

The Knickerbockers

A lot of tinkering took place around 1840, almost all of it on the part of the men's clubs that were popular in America's urban centers. In New York City, a group of young men focused their attention on the game of rounders and added a few wrinkles to make it a little more suitable for adults. Records indicate that they were playing a game called "base ball" sometime in 1842 on open lots in what today would be considered lower midtown Manhattan. In 1845, a bank clerk named Alexander Cartwright suggested they form a proper club, and so it was that the Knickerbocker Base Ball Club—baseball's first "team"—came to be. Like any respectable club of the time, a constitution and extensive rules were drawn up. Because the Knickerbockers were a baseball club, part of these rules pertained to the playing of baseball. Thus, the club's first set of rules are widely regarded as the first rules of baseball, too.

Around this time, the Knickerbockers could no longer find a suitable space to play their game. New York City was growing very quickly during the 1840s, and consequently buildings were being erected in many of the vacant lots the club had used in the past. So rather than traveling far uptown by horse and carriage, they hopped one of the many ferries shuttling back and forth across the Hudson River and went to Hoboken, New Jersey. There the Knickerbockers rented Elysian Field and a nearby dressing room and continued playing their games there. Other men's clubs were also playing baseball at the

time, but it seemed to be a particular favorite of the Knickerbockers. Of course, that did not mean they had the best team. In fact, this would become quite apparent in 1846, when the Knickerbockers played the New York Club in the first recorded game of baseball between two teams. The New York Club won 23-1.

The Knickerbockers were one of hundreds of men's clubs formed on the East Coast during the 1840s and 1850s. Most brought together members of a particular profession— such as bankers, teachers, attorneys, or artisans—and consisted mostly of middle-class workers. These clubs had regular meetings and threw elaborate social affairs. Often the members favored a particular pastime, such as shooting or billiards or, in the case of a few, baseball. Members

A crowd watches the Knickerbockers play an 1846 game at Elysian Field in Hoboken, N.J. Note the location of the umpire, to the right of the catcher.

of the working class (such as manual laborers and factory workers) also had clubs, but they were usually less organized and collected far less money in the form of dues. These organizations often met in saloons, and there is little to suggest they played much baseball in the earliest years of the sport.

The New York Club disappeared from sight after beating the Knickerbockers, and no other baseball-playing clubs challenged the Knickerbockers during the 1840s, so they continued to do what they enjoyed most, dividing members into two "nines" and playing amongst themselves. In 1850, the Washington Club became known around the city for its baseball team, and from 1851 to 1853, the Knickerbockers and the Washingtons played two matches a year. In 1854, the Eagle Club and Empire Club fielded baseball teams, and by 1855 there were 11 baseball-playing clubs in New York and Brooklyn. There were also clubs in Long Island and Newark, New Jersey.

The NABBP

In 1858, under the leadership of the Knickerbockers, a convention of "ball-clubs" was held and the National Association of Base Ball Players (NABBP) was formed. Member clubs agreed to play by the Knickerbocker rules, with one important exception: the Knickerbockers had always played until one team scored 21 runs or "aces," regardless of how many innings it took to do so. When the NABBP was formed, it was agreed that each game would last nine innings, regardless of the score. At the time, this was not viewed as a major difference, for typically it took about nine innings to score that many runs. And game

scores after the rule change often saw both combatants finish with at least 15 to 25 runs. Still, it is hard to imagine what baseball might be like today had the switch from 21 runs to nine innings not been made.

The acceptance of the Knickerbocker rules is perhaps the most compelling reason for recognition of this club as the first true baseball team, for some would argue that others pre-dated them. Philadelphia's Olympic Town Ball Club, for instance, began playing a baseball-like game in 1833. And several clubs in New England had been playing something called the "Massachusetts Game," where the bases were laid out in a square configuration instead of a diamond. What the Knickerbockers, Washingtons, Eagles and other clubs in the New York City area were playing was often called the "New York Game" instead of "baseball." By the 1860s, however, many of the clubs that played variations of Knickerbocker baseball had abandoned their game and joined the NABBP, swelling its membership to more than 50 clubs.

Club Games

The sporting press—which covered boxing, horse racing, sailing, the theater, and, on occasion, sensational crimes—latched on to baseball in the 1850s. They reported on games that took place among the members, and on the rare matches pitting two clubs against each other. There were no leagues or schedules, but on any given afternoon around three o'clock there was usually a "base ball match" being played somewhere in almost every eastern city. These games were covered just as today's games are, except everyone was on the same club. This did not bother baseball fans. In fact, the means by which a club was divided into two teams was often a special point of interest. For instance, one game might find the married members playing against the bachelors, while another might divide players by their age or last initial. Fans enjoyed reading about the contests and followed the progress of certain players, some of whom they knew professionally or socially. Which "team" they happened to be on for the day mattered little.

A baseball game between two clubs was a very special event back in the 1850s and was usually part of an overall day of festivities. For most club members, the highlight of such a meeting would not be the game but the elaborate dinner that followed. This was a spirited social event, highlighted by many speeches and presentations, which often lasted well into the next morning. Indeed, when accounts of games between clubs regularly appeared in the newspapers, they included equally enthusiastic descriptions of the festivities that followed.

On the field, play was generally friendly and courteous during the early 1850s. If an error was committed, the offending player might halt the game to issue an apology. If someone made a good hit or catch, there might be a brief stoppage of play for congratulations. These were the affectations of the early game that made it a "manly" or adult pastime, as opposed to the "boyish" or rowdy contest played by schoolchildren or undignified adults. As one might expect, baseball was a far less demanding sport than it is today. The ball was delivered in an underhand motion, from 45 feet away. A batter could run up and clobber the ball, but it would not go very far because the ball was not tightly constructed. And fielders did not have to run, catch, or throw particularly

well, for any ball caught on one bounce was an automatic out. Even the most uncoordinated player could fend for himself in this game. But that was the basic idea. After so many decades of inactivity, America needed a game that was easy to play.

Although the veneer of baseball in the 1850s was highly social, there were forces at work beneath the surface that would push many clubs to examine the role baseball would play in their affairs. Almost every club had a group of members who were actually good players, and these players became understandably frustrated whenever their less-talented teammates caused them to lose. And it drove them crazy when positions on the team were assigned based on qualifications other than skill. They felt that club should put its nine best men on the field and that there should be practice before games so they could be at their best. By the late 1850s, these individuals were beginning to exert a fair amount of influence on the game. Accounts of matches from this period suggest that pitchers were beginning to throw harder, fielders were making fewer errors and turning more double plays, and runners were stealing bases.

To older club members, who had played baseball during earlier, more innocent times, this sounded like heresy. What would come next? Diving for balls in the outfield? Colliding with basemen on close plays? Deception on the part of the pitcher? They wanted no part of it. Thus by the early 1860s, members of many clubs had become divided over who should be playing baseball and how it should be played. Some clubs went even further. They not only wanted the best players, they were willing to do what had previously been considered unthinkable—pay for their services.

Play for Pay

The idea that money could be made from baseball first became apparent in 1858, during a series of all-star games between New York and Brooklyn players. A nominal fee was charged to attend the game, and more than 5,000 fans showed up, gladly paying their way into the grounds at Brooklyn's Fashion Course. From there, things began to move quickly. Convinced that baseball fans would pay to watch games, club directors began chasing after the best ballplayers. Salaries were against the rules of the NABBP, but clubs got around this by promising to hold benefit games and hand over a share of the profits. By the early 1860s, most of the game's recognized stars—including shortstop Dickey Pearce and James Creighton, the best pitcher of the day—were receiving some sort of regular compensation. Clubs could pay players for intra-club games and not for match play against other clubs, or schedule prize money games against other clubs and apportion large shares to key players if they won.

No one at the time saw the coming of professionalism as being unwanted or unnatural. After all, money and baseball had gone hand-in-hand since the 1840s. Fields had to be rented, equipment purchased, transportation arranged, and admission charged; moreover, gamblers were permanent fixtures in the crowds, openly laying odds for spectators wishing to bet on the outcome of contests. It was up to each club to decide how it would approach baseball. The choices were becoming very clear, and increasingly incompatible—to play the game for recreation or to play to win.

Spreading the Game

The U.S. Civil War, which lasted from 1861 to 1865, changed the course of baseball dramatically. It helped introduce the sport to many young adults who had never played or even seen the game before. Baseball was played quite avidly by Union soldiers be-

PLAY FOR PAY? WHY?

The concept of playing baseball professionally did not appeal to most middle-class men in the 1850s and 1860s. They did not mind playing on a team that included professionals (as long as they behaved themselves), but playing for pay seemed at best slightly absurd and at worst a little sleazy. Most paid performers of the day were either in burlesque, the circus, or the boxing ring.

Why would a club member with a budding career for a respectable company throw that opportunity away to play a silly game? This was not a concern for young men in the lower classes, who faced a lifetime of manual labor and almost no possibility of significant advancement. As one might expect, they brought a no-holds-barred, back-alley flavor to the game.

During the Civil War, Union prisoners play a game of baseball.

tween battles. It was an ideal recreation because it required no equipment other than four bases, a bat, and a ball—all of which could be fashioned from items readily available around a military encampment. Soldiers from the East Coast cities and New England taught the game to the soldiers from western Pennsylvania, Ohio, Michigan, Indiana, and Illinois. Meanwhile, those who were captured in battle and sent to the vast prisoner-of-war compounds in the South taught the game to their Confederate jailers. By the time the war was over, the seeds of baseball had been taken back home and planted in every state in the nation. Consequently, the number of clubs in the NABBP went from a few dozen to nearly 100 in 1865. Fueled by a new kind of aggressiveness and a thirst for victory forged during the war, a different generation of highly skilled players

emerged, and their services were in great demand.

There was a big push to move baseball to a higher level in the late 1860s. Some men's clubs, hoping to field a crack team, had moved away from using legitimate members and turned instead to talented outsiders to represent them. Indeed, by the late 1860s, many teams were made up entirely of paid ballplayers, even though the NABBP's rules still prohibited professionals. The desire to field the best baseball team possible led to a practice called "revolving." Because there were no contracts between clubs and players—and because the best players did not really consider themselves "members" of the clubs they joined—players felt there was no reason why they could not move from one club to another at a moment's notice. They were hired guns, and everyone knew it. What should prevent them from switching teams if they could secure a better salary or a bigger share of gate receipts?

By 1866, there were more than 200 clubs in the NABBP, with much of that growth coming from the midwest and the Baltimore–Washington, D.C., area. Naturally, everyone wanted the best players, the vast majority of whom were still playing in and around New York City. During 1866 and 1867, these players were offered unprecedented financial packages to join teams as far away as Chicago and Cincinnati, and most of them went. This movement of talent, coupled with the fact that New York–area clubs no longer made up a majority in the NABBP, began a shift in power away from the clubs that had first refined and popularized baseball. On the one hand, this was great for baseball, for it signaled the spread of the game across America; on the other hand, the men who ran the NABBP felt the game and its players had suddenly passed them by. Slowly but surely, those who wanted baseball to evolve to an "elite" level wrestled control of the game away from the less aggressive, more socially minded men's clubs that had given birth to organized baseball. By the end of the 1860s, the NABBP was completely out of touch with what was going on in baseball and served no productive purpose.

The Red Stockings

During the summer of 1869, the Cincinnati Red Stockings, a club stocked from top to bottom with professional players, scheduled an unprecedented 56-game national tour. The results of this experiment in professionalism were eye-opening, especially for those in the East who felt that an inferior form of baseball was being played out west. In early June, the Red Stockings beat the powerful Haymakers in Troy, New York, then moved south to play the best clubs in New York City and Brooklyn. Three impressive wins, including one over the Mutuals—widely regarded as the best team of the day—made manager Harry Wright and his team the talk of the baseball world. The Red Stockings ended up winning every game on the tour, raising the bar for other clubs that wanted to compete on baseball's top level.

The 1869 tour was a profitable one for the Red Stockings, and Wright took the team on the road again the following summer. The club dropped six games, however, and lost some of its previous luster. Attendance began to drop off, revenues declined, and the club was faced with rising salary demands. The directors determined that even a wildly successful 1871 tour would still leave the club in debt, which meant its 300-plus members would have their dues raised substantially. In an ironic move, the club decided not to field a professional team anymore. It just was not worth it.

It had finally gotten to the point where a traditional men's club could no longer operate a top team and expect to make a profit. As financially savvy as club members might be, ownership of a successful professional team required a totally new mindset. To generate enough cash to pay the best players, one had to concentrate on something clubs just did not understand: getting fans to pay their way into games. It required a flair for promotion that club members either did not have or felt was somehow beneath them. Like it or not, baseball was becoming a professional sport. And like it or not, professional baseball was becoming part of the entertainment industry.

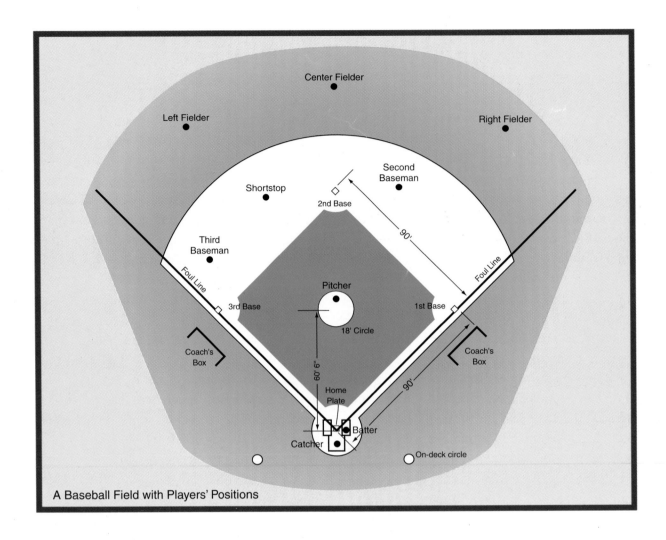

A Baseball Field with Players' Positions

The National Association

The Red Stockings pulled out of professional baseball because the club's directors either lacked the entrepreneurial skills needed to succeed or just did not find the prospect of developing these skills very appealing. This setback did not, however, scare off all of the other clubs. In fact, a group of them banded together over the winter and formed the first baseball league, which they named the National Association of Professional Baseball Players. Play began during the spring of 1871, with the National Association occupying nine cities: New York, Boston, Philadelphia, Cleveland, Washington, D.C., and the smaller towns of Troy, New York; Rockford, Illinois; and Fort Wayne, Indiana. It cost little to join this group—just $10—but even that amount was deemed too expensive by the Brooklyn Eckfords, who sat back and watched the league's first season unfold before joining in 1872.

The class of the National Association was the Boston club, which had secured the services of several top players from the legendary 1869 Cincinnati Red Stockings, as well as two of the game's rising stars in Al Spalding and Ross Barnes. Close behind Boston were the Chicago White Stock-

PLAY BALL!

The first "major-league" game took place on May 4, 1871, between the Forest City Club of Cleveland and the Kekiongas Club of Fort Wayne, whose star pitcher, Bobby Mathews, hurled a 2-0 shutout. It turned out to be the best-pitched game of the season, and Mathews himself went on to become one of the most famous moundsmen of his era, racking up 297 victories in a career that lasted well into the 1880s.

Today's fan would recognize this game as baseball, but there were some interesting differences. Mathews was throwing from just 45 feet away, and he was not throwing from a mound, but from a level, six-foot square box. The batter stood with one foot on each side of a line drawn through home plate, and he could call for a pitch above or below the waist. It took three strikes to strike a batter out, but strikes were awfully hard to come by. Foul balls, for instance, did not count as strikes; and the first good pitch a batter took was not called a strike by the umpire, who usually issued a warning that he had better swing at the next one in that location.

Was National Association baseball a hitter's game? Not really. In baseball's early years, a pitch that was not called a strike was not automatically a ball. Typically, an umpire would warn a pitcher several times that he had better throw a fair pitch before calling balls. The rule was meant more to prevent the delaying of a game than to award a batter first base. But once an umpire began calling pitches outside the strike zone, it only took three balls for a batter to draw a walk. What if a pitcher nailed a hitter with an inside pitch? It was the batter's tough luck. He was given a few moments to collect himself and then ordered back up to bat!

The bases were a little different than they are today. First base and third base straddled the foul lines. Thus a ball hit down the line could pass over the base and still technically be foul. By contrast, a ball that touched fair territory and then spun foul was considered fair. The hot grounders that skip foul by a foot or two today were fair balls back then, meaning the first and third basemen had to play close to the line. This opened up huge holes in the infield, putting added pressure on the shortstop and second baseman. There was added pressure on the cornermen, too, for home plate in the 1870s was a square slab of stone; a crafty hitter could bang a pitch straight down off the edge of the plate and send it ricocheting off at an odd angle into what today would be foul territory. Some fielders actually positioned themselves in foul territory to prevent this very play.

Mathews' catcher, Bill Lennon, wore no mask or chest protector and did not have a glove or shin guards; none of these items had been invented yet. Of course, Lennon was not crazy. He stood a safe distance behind the plate, as did the game's lone umpire, who called the entire game from foul territory, including tag plays at second base and shoestring catches in the outfield. Occasionally, catcher and umpire were joined by a third player—a substitute—who would run for an injured batter after he hit the ball.

Unlike today, pitching was not a team's primary means of defense. With the exception of four or five hard-to-hit hurlers, most pitchers simply delivered the ball to the plate and got out of the way when the batter swung. That meant an awful lot hinged on infielders and outfielders, which was something of a problem, because fielding during this time was not a pretty thing to watch. No one wore a glove, and by the middle of a game both the ball and the field could get pretty chewed up. This led to a lot of errors, often several in one inning, and consequently to a lot of scoring. Teams batted roughly what they do today—.240 to .280—but because of the many miscues a typical game score was more likely to be 15-8 than 3-1.

There was not a lot of science to hitting back then. Batters generally swung from the heels and tried to hit the ball as hard and as far as they could. The ball's innards, made of yarn, were not wrapped very tightly, and thus even a perfectly met pitch did not travel more than 350 feet before coming to earth. Outfielders got to most of the balls hit their way, but they did not always catch them. Line drives at infielders were as good as hits and would remain so until gloves with webbing were introduced decades later. As for base running, it was quite similar to what it is today, as the bases were 90 feet apart. Base-running strategy was still developing, however, and it would be several years before sliding became a common practice and several more before base stealing evolved into a key offensive weapon.

ings—led by pitcher George Zettlein, whose underhand delivery was the fastest in baseball—and the Philadelphia Athletics, whose 31-year-old second baseman, Al Reach, would one day build a sporting-goods empire.

As the season wore on, the inevitable problems of a new league began to pop up. Chief among them was the matter of the standings. Then, as now, a team would play a series of games when it came to a city, after which it would either return home or move on to the next city. In the National Association, these series lasted five games.

But there was never a clear understanding of whether they were best-of-five meetings or simple, straightforward five-game affairs. If one team won three of three or three of four, should the remaining games count in the standings? No one could agree, and the bylaws of the association were not clear on this matter. Imagine the confusion when fans opened one newspaper to see the White Stockings in first place, only to find the Red Stockings commanding the top spot in another newspaper. In fact, it was not entirely clear whether the league's eventual champion would be the club that won the most games or the most series. In the end the Athletics, with an official record of 22–7, were awarded the Association crown.

The National Association was in operation for five seasons, and during that time four important developments occurred in baseball. First, the focus of the game shifted from the country's midsection back to the East Coast. Harry Wright took his best players from Cincinnati and formed the Boston Red Stockings, who reeled off four straight championships beginning in 1872. Also, three midwestern franchises folded and were replaced by eastern clubs. Second, the money-making potential of organized baseball had become crystal clear. A well-run team could turn a tidy profit if it put a good product on the field. The only drawbacks to team ownership were the instability of other franchises and the ease with which players could move from team to team. If another club folded and you happened to have them scheduled for an upcoming series, you were out the gate receipts but still on the hook for player salaries. And as far as player salaries were concerned, you needed to pay top dollar for top players, and there was practically nothing to prevent them from signing up with a rival club. Third, the players—by virtue of their freedom of movement—had far too much power to enable organized baseball to thrive and evolve as a profitable entity. The National Association of Professional Baseball Players was just that: an association of ballplayers. They played the games; they made the rules; they made the money. If a gambler offered a player a few bucks to make a bad throw at a key moment, there was nothing to stop him from doing so. If a player felt like stopping in a saloon for a few drinks before a ball game, there was little a club owner could do when he

showed up drunk. This situation did not sit well with those who had bigger plans for pro baseball. Fourth, the game grew tremendously in its national appeal from 1871 to 1875, thanks to the emergence and promotion of its stars. Names that might never have been uttered outside of a city's borders were now in print around the country, along with their impressive statistics.

Ironically, it was a combination of these elements that actually spelled doom for the National Association. Hoping to capitalize on the growing popularity of professional baseball, six new teams joined the association for the 1875 season, swelling its ranks to 13. Five of the new teams quickly proved unable to compete against the established clubs, and as the Red Stockings began to pull away from the pack for a fourth straight year, interest in many cities waned and clubs began to fold right and left. This left the remaining clubs in a terrible bind, for each game canceled meant the loss of that day's gate receipts.

The tilting of power from west back to east also created problems, which came to a head in the matter of Davy Force. Force had starred for the Chicago White Stockings the season before, and as the rules of the time permitted, spent the winter negotiating with both Chicago and the Philadelphia Athletics. But then he signed contracts with both clubs, which was definitely against the rules. It was up to the Association's Judiciary Committee to determine Force's fate, and it ruled in favor of the White Stockings, for the slippery little shortstop had signed their contract first. A few months later the Association elected a new president, who happened to be a native Philadelphian. He in turn appointed a new Judiciary Committee. Incredibly, they overturned the former

William Hulbert (above) founded the National League in 1876.

committee's decision and awarded Force to the Athletics!

William Hulbert, who financed the Chicago club, was furious. He contacted some of the National Association's other financial backers and began to lay plans for a new organization. Hulbert envisioned a league of professional baseball teams that would be run professionally—not by the players but by the owners. They would treat clubs like businesses, and players would be little more than corporate assets. Hulbert's fellow investors thought the idea sounded fine. They had had enough of the National Association. By early summer, the plan was set in motion. Taking full advantage of the lax rules that had so frustrated him, Hulbert approached Boston's top players—Spalding, Barnes, McVey, and White—and signed them for the following season. When word got out the four were labeled traitors, and the club was expected to fall apart. But they kept right on winning, finishing the year 18 games ahead of the second-place Hartford Dark Blues. Later in the season, Hulbert signed young Adrian "Cap" Anson to a deal, too.

The National League

Early in 1876—about a month before the regular National Association meeting—Hulbert arranged a meeting of his own, inviting representatives from seven of the clubs to discuss the instability of club finances, remedies for game-fixing, and rules that were not working as planned. After they filed into the room he rented at the Grand Central Hotel, Hulbert locked the door behind the men, slipped the key into his pocket, and told them the real reason he had called them to New York on that cold February day: He was inviting them to join him in the formation of a new and radically different baseball league.

The founding principle of the proposed league was simple and straightforward. Players would have no say whatsoever in club or league finances and would hold no position above the post of field manager. Such a structure, Hulbert claimed, would make baseball a much more stable financial investment, as well as a cleaner game, since owners could mete out any punishment they saw fit for substandard play, drunkenness, and consorting with gamblers. Hulbert also told his "captive" audience that the league would take the game of baseball to a higher moral level, eventually appealing to the high-class sports fans who might pay double the present 25-cents admission if they could be guaranteed an environment free from the drunken riffraff and petty thieves who many believed attended ball games. In its quest for respectability, the league would not allow beer or whiskey into its ballparks, there would be no Sunday games, and cursing by the players would not be tolerated. And although teams would be competing against one another, team owners would be cooperating behind-the-scenes as partners to ensure competitive balance—something the Association sorely lacked. This new arrangement would not only funnel a higher percentage of profits into their pockets, Hulbert insisted, it would also work toward the betterment of the game. It sounded like a pretty good deal—certainly better than the one that awaited them with another season backing Association clubs. By the time Hulbert let his fellow investors out, the National League of Baseball Clubs was born and the National Association of Professional Baseball Players was no more.

As the National League began its inaugural season in 1876, the players did not realize at first how much they were about to lose. The teams had the same names, and the same fellows seemed to be running things. And in their minds, it was business as usual in terms of hooking up with a team, negotiating a contract, pulling on a uniform, and playing the game. And indeed it was, for the first few years of the new league. Although the process was a bit more businesslike, players continued to move from team to team with relative freedom, and the top stars were paid handsomely for their services, whether they stayed put or took their talents to another team.

But all was not well in baseball. The New York Mutuals and Philadelphia Athletics were unceremoniously booted out of the league by Hulbert after refusing to play their last few road games. The clubs were out of contention, short on cash, and still used to the old rules of the National Association. With the National League down to six teams, the schedule was reduced from 70 to 60 games in 1877. In an attempt to attract more fans, admission was dropped from 50 cents to a dime after the third inning, and clubs were allowed to make extra money by playing each other in unofficial exhibitions, usually on Wednesdays and Fridays. These changes, done with an eye toward building fan loyalty, were later undone when it was discovered that four players on the Louisville Grays had conspired to throw games during the heat of the pennant race. The offending players were immediately banned for life, and the Louisville franchise folded. So, too, did the St. Louis franchise, which was also implicated in the scandal. The Hartford Dark Blues also folded their tent, failing to draw fans even after relocating to Brooklyn, traditionally a baseball hotbed. Thus the 1878 season started with just three of the National League's original eight franchises still intact.

More franchises came and went during the league's third and fourth campaigns, and a new league called the International Association had grown enough in strength and quality of play to become a real headache to National League owners. It was beginning to look like Hulbert's dream of clean and profitable baseball was just that: a dream. For his part, Hulbert had kept his word and ruled the game firmly and fairly, but his promises of increased profitability had not come true for any club other than his own. That he was the shrewdest, most visionary of the owners made no matter to his peers; as they had understood it back at that dramatic locked-door meeting, in Hulbert's new league even an idiot was guaranteed to make a profit. The problem was that Americans were playing baseball, but they were not shelling out their hard-earned money to see it.

The Reserve Clause

Given the state of baseball at the end of the 1870s, how could the owners make their teams more profitable? The answer came out of Boston, where co-owner Arthur Soden dreamed up a clever way to keep the league's poorer clubs competitive. Even though the Red Caps, as the Boston team was then called, were one of the elite franchises, Soden recognized that the annual demise of the league's weaker members threatened to destroy everything the National League was striving for. Soden proposed to his fellow owners that each team be allowed to "reserve" the services of five players for the following season, and that other teams could not negotiate with these individuals. That meant a cellar-dwelling team, desperate for cash, would not have to outbid the wealthier clubs just to keep its few decent players. It sounded like a sensible suggestion, and the reserve rule was

THE RESERVE CLAUSE

As originally put forth, the reserve rule was a way of letting teams develop and keep star players, and thus maintain a competitive balance. But soon its real value became clear to everyone. With the top 40 players out of circulation that winter, there was little left for the owners to fight over. It had not been the players driving up costs with greater and greater salary demands; it was the owners who were blowing their own budgets by trying to outbid one another for the game's top stars. The reserve rule essentially kept them from cutting their own throats!

Now that the owners had found a way to curb their escalating expenses, what was to keep them from purposely driving salaries down? Actually, nothing. If a reserved player did not like what an owner was offering he had but two choices: quit baseball or go play for some semipro outfit in the middle of nowhere for next to nothing. A wave of massive salary cuts and trumped-up fines ensued, and the players were furious. Ironically, at first they had gladly signed contracts according them a "reserved" status. They thought of it as a mark of excellence. But they quickly realized that they were at the complete mercy of their employers. Anyone who doubted the seriousness of the owners had only to look at the plight of Boston's Charley Jones, the National League's batting champ just the year before. When a minor salary squabble escalated into a series of bogus fines and suspensions, Jones left the team and was never permitted to play in the league again.

voted into the NL bylaws. Two days later, the International Association folded, meaning that for the time being the National League was the only game in town.

The economy perked up in 1880, bringing more fans into the ballparks than ever before. Lower salaries and greater attendance put many clubs into the black for the first time, and Hulbert was beginning to look like a genius. One team, however, was still struggling to compete. The Cincinnati Red Stockings (who borrowed their name from the great club of 1869) broke one of Hulbert's golden rules by permitting Sunday baseball and by selling alcohol on the premises. After the season, Hulbert threw the Red Stockings out of the National League, admitting the Detroit Wolverines in their place.

The 1881 season brought prosperity and competitive balance to the National League. It also saw batting averages soar, thanks to a new rule that moved the pitcher's box from 45 to 50 feet from home plate. For the second straight year, Hulbert's Chicago White Stockings proved the best team in the league. Player-manager Cap Anson led the NL in hits, RBIs, batting, and slugging, while rightfielder King Kelly blossomed into a terrific all-around player. The pitching tandem of Larry Corcoran and Fred Goldsmith turned in their second straight superb season, combining for 55 wins and nine shutouts.

The White Stockings won the pennant with relative ease, but for the first time in a long time nearly every team competed in a pitched battle for the next few spots. The new Detroit franchise played splendid baseball and finished fourth despite a roster of unknown and marginally talented players. The Buffalo Bisons snagged a third-place finish thanks to a fine season from star pitcher Pud Galvin, the acquisition of veterans Deacon White and Jim O'Rourke, and a breakthrough offensive year from emerging superstar Dan Brouthers. In second place were the Providence Grays, who got a huge year from rookie Charley "Hoss" Radbourn. He used a screwball to win 25 games and turned in a league-best .694 winning percentage. He also introduced the idea of tossing a few warm-up pitches before each inning began. Even the last-place Worcester Ruby Legs made a go of things in 1881. Thanks to the aggressive style of first baseman Harry Stovey—one of the first players to slide feet-first—and the rubber arm of 25-game winner Lee Richmond, the team won almost 40 percent of its games. Indeed, the level of play had never been higher in baseball. Still, if a player hoped to make it as a pro, the National League was the only game in town.

The American Association

That situation changed dramatically the following spring, when a rival league, the American Association (AA), set up shop in six major American cities: Philadelphia, Louisville, Pittsburgh, St. Louis, Baltimore, and Cincinnati. None of these cities had National League teams, but the American Association did go head-to-head with the established circuit in its attempt to win over fans the NL had ignored. By charging a lower admission price, scheduling contests for Sundays, and permitting liquor to be served at games, the Association threw its arms open to working-class people in these working-class towns. The idea was not to lure established NL stars into jumping their

The cover of this 1884 book, *Sports and Pastimes of American Boys*, shows youngsters playing baseball (middle panel).

gloveless, in the pitcher's box, with both hands on the ball, and then fire it toward the batter with either hand. He was also one of the game's first switch-hitters. The muscular, handsome Mullane was a great favorite around the league, earning the nickname "Apollo of the Box."

After the 1882 season, the National League and American Association scrambled to put new teams in the unoccupied cities of New York and Philadelphia. With East Coast–hating Hulbert dead, there was nothing to stop the NL from claiming these prizes, and it did so by transferring the Troy and Worcester franchises. And so the New York Gothams and Philadelphia Quakers—forerunners of today's Giants and Phillies—were born. The new AA teams were called the New York Metropolitans, or Mets, and the Philadelphia Athletics. Other than vying for fans in these key cities, the two leagues agreed to stay out of each other's way as much as possible. At a February meeting, each vowed to honor the other's contracts, and they expanded the reserve clause to cover 11 men instead of only five. The American Association may have created more jobs for hitters and pitchers, but it was also a willing accomplice when it came to tightening baseball's grip on those who played the game.

The relationship between the two leagues was downright cozy by this time, especially when it came to keeping a foot on the throat of the players. During the 1885 season, they conspired to create a salary cap of $2,000 per player, although few owners were brave enough to stick to it when it came time to re-sign their stars for 1886. The mere thought of a salary cap, however, was enough to make the players organize themselves for the first time. John Ward, the star shortstop for the

teams but to tap into the talent that had gone undiscovered.

The Chicago White Stockings won the National League pennant again in 1882, and the Cincinnati Red Stockings—essentially the same team Hulbert kicked out of the NL in 1880—took the Association flag. The AA's biggest star that first season was Tony Mullane of the third-place Louisville Eclipse. Mullane, who was cut after a lackluster rookie season with the Detroit Wolverines, hooked on with the Eclipse and became the Association's most durable pitcher. It stood to reason that he could go longer and stronger than other hurlers, for Mullane was ambidextrous. He would stand

THE FIRST WORLD SERIES

At the end of the 1882 season, the two league champions met in Cincinnati for an impromptu championship series in order to make some extra money. Cap Anson, assuming the Red Stockings were merely a pumped-up version of the team that had finished in the National League cellar in 1880, played his best pitcher, Larry Corcoran, at shortstop and did not even bother to bring King Kelly to the game.

The Red Stockings, behind 40-game winner Will White, trounced the haughty Chicagoans 4-0. Besides winning what was essentially the first "World Series" game, White, the younger brother of catching star Deacon White, was also the first major leaguer to wear sunglasses on the field. In the second game of the series, Anson sent Corcoran to the mound, where he blanked the Reds 2-0. Again, White was magnificent, allowing just four hits, with the two runs scoring on a pair of first-inning errors. The game was most notable for the way in which Chicago scored its first run. With the speedy George Gore on first, Anson called for a steal of second, while at the same time instructing slugger Ned Williamson to push the ball through the spot vacated by second baseman Bid McPhee. It was an early version of the hit-and-run. Although it would not become a common weapon in baseball for at least another decade, it proved to be the deciding factor in this contest. Williamson executed perfectly, rolling the ball out to cannon-armed right-fielder Harry Wheeler, who promptly threw the ball into the stands trying to cut down Gore, who was on his way to third base. A deciding game was never played between the two teams. Chicago had already agreed to play National League runner-up Providence in a post-season series, and American Association president Denny McKnight, who felt exhibition contests were an invitation to game-fixing on the part of players, wired a threat of expulsion to Cincinnati if they did not end the series immediately.

newly renamed New York Giants, got the support of top players Buck Ewing and Tim Keefe and formed the Brotherhood of Professional Baseball Players.

The Players League

In the fall of 1889, Ward announced the formation of a third major league, which he christened the Players League. The teams would not be owned by the players, but the bylaws abolished the salary cap, the reserve clause, and the right to trade a player without his permission. Everyone would work on a one-year contract, with another option year if the club wished to retain a player's services. If not, he would be free to negotiate with any club he chose. The Players

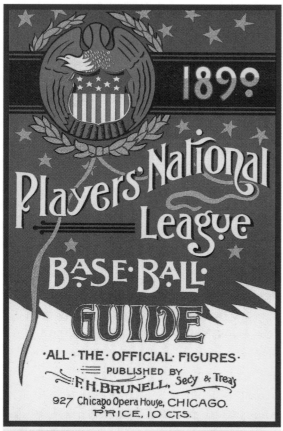

The 1890 *Players League Guide* provided statistics and information about the league's first and only season.

League did not serve alcohol in its parks or schedule Sunday games. This was a great relief to the American Association, which was still the only league that catered to the working-class fan. The Players League set up shop in eight cities, only one of which— Buffalo—did not already have at least one major league team.

It might have been an interesting three-way battle had a power struggle not occurred within the American Association prior to the 1890 season. A squabble over the election of a new league president caused the 1889 pennant-winning Brooklyn Bridegrooms to pull out and join the National League. With them went the Cincinnati Reds, Baltimore Orioles, and Kansas City Cowboys. The Association's misfortunes mounted further when a national crusade was launched by Sabbatarians to prevent Sunday baseball. They disrupted games in every city, and baseball fans eventually found something else to do on Sundays instead of attending AA games.

With the American Association gasping for air, the real battle in the summer of 1890 was between the National League and the Players League. Ward's circuit put a better brand of baseball on the field, and for the most part beat the NL at the turnstiles. By season's end, the Brooklyn Bridegrooms— the first team to use a three-man pitching rotation—were the National League champions. The Association flag went to the Louisville Colonels, who had finished dead last the season before. They probably owed their triumph to the fact that none of their veterans were talented enough to be of interest to raiders from the Players League.

The Players League pennant was won by the Boston Reds, who got great offensive years out of leftfielder Hardy Richardson, first baseman Dan Brouthers, and right-fielder Harry Stovey. Hoss Radbourn anchored a pitching staff that included 23-game winner Ad Gumbert and Matt Kilroy, who had once been baseball's supreme strikeout artist. All of the top players came through, including Pete Browning, who won the batting title for the Cleveland Infants, and New York's Roger Connor, who added to his stature as the 19th-century's most feared slugger by blasting 14 home runs.

In almost every respect, the Players League was a roaring success. The one

THE UNION ASSOCIATION

Ironically, the loudest outcry over the expanded reserve clause came not from the players, but from a wealthy St. Louis banker named Henry Lucas, who felt the reserve clause was nothing short of slavery. Indentured servitude was still a touchy issue in the United States because the Civil War was still fresh in the national memory, and the Reconstruction process in the former Confederacy had been anything but smooth. Lucas took it upon himself to remedy the evils of baseball by forming his own league and inviting players and investors to join him in a glorious experiment. So for the 1884 season, baseball fans actually had three leagues from which to choose: the National League, the American Association, and the new Union Association. To make things even more complicated, the American Association expanded into Brooklyn, Indianapolis, Toledo, and Washington, D.C. The AA sought to gain footholds in these cities, fearing the Union Association might move in first. The result was a confusing, uninteresting tangle of teams, leagues, and cities.

Lucas, who owned the St. Louis Maroons, scheduled his first 11 games against the Altoona Mountain Citys, the worst team in the league. The Maroons won them all, and took their next nine for good measure to start the season 20–0. It did wonders for Lucas's ego but killed any fan interest in the new league, as St. Louis ran off with the pennant. By the summer, many Union Association teams had folded, while others had moved to new cities. Prior to the 1885 season, Lucas was invited to join the National League and he accepted. When the other Union Association owners saw this, they disbanded the league.

place it did not succeed, however, was on the ledger sheet. Several of the franchises were on the verge of bankruptcy, and the remaining owners were afraid they might lose their shirts if they went through another season like 1890. What they did not know was that many more teams in the other two leagues were in far worse shape! In fact, had the Players league forged ahead, it would most likely have collapsed the American Association and sent the National League into a financial tailspin. With a little more nerve and another year of experience, the Players League might well have become the dominant major league and changed the very course of professional sports in this country. But early in 1891, the Players League quietly decided to end its great experiment after only one season.

As it turned out, the 1891 season was the American Association's last. In December, the two leagues agreed to merge, with the National League continuing operation as a 12-team circuit that for many years was referred to as the "League-Association." Although the American Association "lost" its war with the National League, its influence was clear in the new look of major-league baseball. Eight of the 12 NL teams had once been Association franchises, and a great many of the game's top stars developed in the junior league. More significantly, perhaps, the National League rewrote its rules so that teams could play games on Sundays if the local laws allowed and sell liquor at their ballparks if they so chose. And any team that wanted to boost attendance with 25-cent ticket prices was free to do so. With all of the competition out of the way, the National League's 12 owners had themselves what every business owner wanted in the 1890s, a monopoly. They could do whatever they wanted, charge whatever they wanted, and treat anyone anyway they pleased. They knew how to wield this power, too. For unlike some of the small-time hustlers and unscrupulous characters who owned clubs during the 1870s and 1880s, this group of owners was experienced and ruthless when it came to running a business.

The Modern Game

It was during the 1890s that baseball truly began to resemble the modern game. The vast majority of pitchers were throwing overhand or sidearm; catchers were beginning to play right up behind the batter; and just about every player was using a glove. After years of adjusting the number of balls and strikes for a walk or strikeout, the National Commission settled on the four-ball/three-strike ratio that remains to this day. In 1893, the commission decided to move pitchers back 10 feet, from 50 feet

to 60 feet. By the time the game's groundskeepers received their instructions, however, a printer's error had changed 60' 0" to 60' 6". When this error was discovered, it was too late to do anything, for hundreds of fields around the country had already been altered. This mistake was never corrected, and it remains the official distance separating pitcher and batter. Other important developments included the balk rule, which prevented a pitcher from faking his delivery and then trying to pick-off an unwary runner, and the infield fly rule, which prevented an infielder from purposely dropping a pop-up with men on base so he could start a double play. By the end of the decade, most ballparks were painting the centerfield fence a dark color to give batters a better hitting background, and in 1901, home plate changed from a four-sided shape to its present form.

Of all these developments, the one with the most pronounced effect on baseball was the new pitching distance. Contrary to popular belief, pitchers were not actually releasing the ball 10 feet further away. It was more like five, because a rule that had already been in place for six seasons kept a pitcher's back foot behind a line 55' 6" from home plate. The real killer was that this line had been replaced by a rubber slab, and hurlers were now required to keep their back foot in contact with it until they released the ball. Those who moved around a lot in the old box, or who liked to take a running start before firing the ball toward home plate, had to relearn their craft. Some small advantages were given back to the pitchers, including the abolishment of flat-sided bats (which made it easier to purposely foul off pitches) and the establishment of the pitcher's mound. Not surprisingly, the dominant pitchers during the 1890s featured blazing fastballs, but only a couple managed to last as power pitchers over the long haul. The rest of the hurlers took a long time to adjust, and while they did the batters enjoyed a feast of hittable pitches.

Indeed, no fewer than seven different players topped the .400 mark during the 1890s. New records for hits, doubles, triples, runs, total bases, and extra-base hits were made and re-made during the decade, despite the fact that field conditions and defensive play were steadily improving. Among the brightest hitting stars of the time were sluggers Ed Delehanty and Sam Thompson, speedy Billy Hamilton of the Phillies, and Chicago's five-tool standout (with the ability to hit, hit with power, run, field, and throw) Bill Lange. The Cleveland Spiders boasted an offensive machine in leftfielder Jesse Burkett, as well as one of history's best-hitting double-play combinations in shortstop Ed McKean and second baseman Cupid Childs.

Hall-of-Famer Charles "Kid" Nichols was baseball's first power pitcher.

The Beaneaters and the Orioles

The rest of the National League's big stars were concentrated on the two dominant teams of the era, the Boston Beaneaters and the Baltimore Orioles. The Beaneaters captured the 1891 pennant by reeling off 18 straight wins to overtake Cap Anson's Chicago Colts in a wild September race, thanks to the pitching of veterans John Clarkson and Harry Staley and the blazing fastball of 21-year-old Charles Nichols, whom everyone called "Kid." Nichols belonged to a new breed of pitcher who preferred to overpower hitters rather than ruin

their timing with different speeds and locations. He was again the key when the Beaneaters took the 1892 pennant and proved even more important in Boston's third straight league title in 1893. With the pitching distance moved back, Boston's number two and three starters got shelled, but Nichols kept right on mowing down opponents. His strikeout totals dipped, but he was still getting hitters out and keeping runs from crossing the plate.

The offense during these three championship seasons was anchored by outfielders Hugh Duffy and Tommy McCarthy and by third baseman Billy Nash. This trio did not overpower opponents as much as they manufactured runs. They made the hit-and-run play an effective and dangerous weapon and just about perfected the double steal. Shortstop Herman Long was a great defensive player, and outfielder Bobby Lowe was one of the best power hitters of his time; but on paper, the Beaneaters certainly did not look like a dynasty. Credit for that went to manager Frank Selee, who could judge ability and read his players well enough to get the absolute best out of each. When age and injury ended Boston's three-year run, Selee transformed backup catcher Fred Tenney into the league's slickest-fielding first baseman, taught Lowe how to play second base, and plucked 25-year-old rookie Jimmy Collins off the last-place Louisville Colonels to play beside the veteran Long. Out of nothing, Selee had produced the best infield in history to that time, and the Beaneaters—with Nichols still firing fastballs past hitters—won the pennant again in 1897 and 1898.

The Beaneater resurgence in the late 1890s was welcomed as a victory for the good guys, because from 1894 to 1896, the National League was dominated by the dark cloud known as the Baltimore Orioles. The Orioles would do anything—absolutely anything—to win. Like Boston, Baltimore maximized the talents of its players and excelled in the game's most exotic strategies. But the Orioles did not stop there. They verbally and physically intimidated umpires and opponents. The Orioles played as hard as they could within the rules, and if that was not enough, they cheated.

The Orioles dynasty was made up almost entirely of players hand-picked by manager Ned Hanlon. No one in history has ever turned so little into so much. Hanlon started with a core of players from Balti-

more's days as an American Association franchise. He had a pugnacious little third baseman named John McGraw, a clever, slap-hitting catcher named Wilbert Robinson, and Sadie McMahon, the AA's top winner in 1890 and 1891. The Orioles manager then took advantage of a maneuver that, until the 1890s, was not all that common, the trade. In the two years preceding the team's first pennant, Hanlon picked up outfielder Joe Kelley from Pittsburgh, obtained a weak-hitting shortstop named Hughie Jennings from the Louisville Colonels, and managed to pry outfielder Steve Brodie away from the St. Louis Browns. He also acquired Dan Brouthers, who looked to be over-the-hill after a sluggish 1893 season, and the Bridegrooms threw in an unknown outfielder named Willie Keeler. Hanlon was a tremendous motivator, and he drilled his team until their execution was perfect. Then he conveyed the simple, straightforward message that they were to do whatever it took to win or they would quickly find themselves where he had found them, on baseball's scrap heap.

In 1894, Baltimore's fielding was superb, its hitting timely, and its base running ferocious; the team caught the NL totally off-guard with its dirty tactics. Although offensive production was up all around the league that season, no team had more players produce breakout years than the Orioles. Kelley played an exceptional centerfield and nearly batted .400. Keeler, who was barely big enough to hit the ball 300 feet, directed single after single through unoccupied spots in the infield and dumped countless balls in front of frustrated outfielders—no matter how teams defensed him, he managed to find a way to cross them up, finishing the year with a .371 aver-

The 1896 Baltimore Orioles pose for a team picture. The down-and-dirty Orioles dominated the National League in the mid-1890s.

age and 165 runs scored. Brodie was second on the club to Keeler in hits, and batted .366. Brouthers had indeed slowed down a step, but he still managed to drive home a team-high 128 runs and collect 71 extra-base hits to go along with his .347 average. Even Jennings proved an enthusiastic pupil of Baltimore's style, and he slashed his way to a .335 average and 37 steals. When the league's other contenders sagged slightly in the final six weeks, Hanlon's band of cut-throats went for the jugular and finished off the season with 28 wins in their last 31 contests and edged the Giants by three games.

For all the heroics provided by sluggers like Brouthers and Kelley, the heart and soul of this team was unquestionably John McGraw. He proved the supreme opportunist, reaching base on sheer will sometimes and scoring in a dozen different ways. All but 33 of his 174 hits in 1894 were singles, yet he still managed to rack up an amazing 156 runs. When opposing hurlers began to pitch around cleanup man Kelley and the Orioles began to slump, the weak-hitting McGraw took his slot and got the team going again. And it was McGraw who inspired the team to a repeat performance in 1895, even though he was suffering from malaria. Despite missing 35 games, he managed to drag himself around the bases 110 times and still led the team with 61 steals. How McGraw, in his weakened condition, batted .369 is anyone's guess. The Orioles

Orioles third baseman John McGraw shows his batting grip. He later managed the New York Giants to 10 pennants in 30 years (1902–32).

won their third straight pennant in 1896, with essentially the same cast of characters, and seemed on course to win a fourth in 1897 before the players got bored fighting opponents, umpires, and fans and instead began pummeling each other.

The Orioles might have become a dynasty had their owner, Henry Von der Horst, not become greedy. In 1899, several owners began discussing the possibility of co-owning two teams and loading up the one in the larger market with the best players in order to maximize attendance. That they had no regard for the competitive balance of their sport is typical of the way big business thought in the 1890s; the product was not nearly as important as the bottom line. Von der Horst, frustrated by the drop in revenues that accompanied his team's fall to second place in 1897 and 1898, cut a deal with Brooklyn owner Fred Abell to send his best players to Brooklyn. Off to the Bridegrooms went Jennings, Keeler, Kelley, Hanlon, and several other key players. The plan succeeded, as Brooklyn doubled its attendance and ran away with the NL pennant, but it decimated the once-mighty Orioles.

Back in Baltimore, John McGraw acted as player-manager and coaxed a surprising 86 wins out of an uninspiring group of players. He led the league in walks and runs scored, did some good teaching, and managed to cull a couple of young stars—pitcher Joe McGinnity and speedy outfielder Jimmy Sheckard—from a roster that saw 32 players come and go that summer.

Turn of the Century

The first season of the new century was an important one for baseball. The National League had consolidated to eight teams, and the level of play was superb. Most of the league's franchises were making money, and fans were treated to a good mix of rising stars and well-known veterans. Honus Wagner blossomed for the Pirates, leading the league in doubles, triples, batting, and slugging. Joe McGinnity repeated his fine performance of 1899 with 28 wins after transferring to Brooklyn when the Baltimore franchise was dropped. He teamed with Lave Cross, Fielder Jones and Jimmy Sheckard—as well as ex-Oriole veterans Keeler, Kelley, and Jennings—to lead the Bridegrooms to a second straight NL championship.

Outfielders Elmer Flick and Roy

CY YOUNG

Although pitchers during the 19th century did not throw as hard as today's hurlers, they did throw a lot more pitches over the course of a season and enjoyed far less rest between starts. Not surprisingly, a typical pitcher suffered some sort of injury within a few years of making the big leagues. And because there was almost no knowledge of sports medicine, these injuries rarely healed. The first pitcher who defied these odds was Denton Young, whose nickname "Cy" was short for cyclone. The Cleveland Spiders righthander did not exactly hit the league like a tornado, but he had a live fastball and near-perfect control.

With a good offensive team behind him for most of the 1890s, he was able to top 20 wins nine times and reached 30 on three occasions. Young was never really the best pitcher of his day—an amusing fact considering that the award for best pitcher is now named in his honor—but he was right up there in the top five for most of the decade. What made Young so wondrous was his longevity; he never suffered any of the injuries that seemed to end every other pitcher's career. Like Nolan Ryan some eight decades later, his mechanics and physique meshed perfectly, reducing the stress on his arm and shoulder and enabling him to mow down hitters well into his 40s.

The second half of Young's career found him in Boston, where he led the American League in wins his first three seasons. Young finally called it quits in 1911, even though he still could get the ball up to the plate in the high 80s. His legs were shot, and he could no longer field his position. In the end, "Old Cy," winner of 511 major-league games, was quite literally bunted out of baseball.

Thomas emerged as stars for the Phillies, joining Ed Delehanty and Napoleon Lajoie, who were already established as two of the top players in the game. St. Louis saw second-year outfielder Mike Donlin blossom into a consistent hitter and got good performances out of veterans Jesse Burkett, Cy Young, and John McGraw, who once again found a way to lead the league in on-base percentage. The Chicago Orphans (they were not yet the Cubs) had lost Bill Lange when his wife made him quit baseball for a more respectable profession; but perennial 20-game winner Clark Griffith was still getting batters out, and a young, slick-fielding third sacker named Bill Bradley was the talk of the town. In Boston, the Beaneaters were quietly assembling the makings of another great team, adding slugger Buck Freeman and pitcher Bill Dineen from the defunct Washington Nationals to a squad of established veterans, including Jimmy Collins, Hugh Duffy, Chick Stahl, Billy Hamilton, and Herman Long.

This 1904 card depicts a dapper young Connie Mack. The gentlemanly Mack managed the Philadelphia Athletics for 50 years.

The American League

With this embarrassment of riches came the inevitable threat from a rival league. Back in the early 1890s when the American Association and Players League folded, many major leaguers sought employment in the Western League, a recently established minor league. With this influx of talent, and under the shrewd and imaginative guidance of a young businessman named Ban Johnson, the Western League became the strongest pro circuit outside the NL. Johnson got an important hand from Charlie Comiskey, who retired from a decade-long

career as a player-manager with the Browns and Red Stockings and took over the Sioux City franchise, which he moved from Iowa to St. Paul, Minnesota. The two men built up the league's prestige and stocked its teams with capable players, all the while with an eye toward acquiring major-league status one day. In 1900, they renamed their venture the American League and moved teams into Chicago, Boston, and Philadelphia, where they went up against NL franchises. The American League also shifted clubs into large cities that had been abandoned or ignored by the NL, including Detroit, Milwaukee, Cleveland, Baltimore, and Washington, D.C.

After making it through one season under this alignment, Johnson stepped up his assault on the National League by encouraging AL owners to offer the NL's best players huge contracts to join the new league. The $2,400 salary cap was still very much in effect in the National League, so it was easy to entice most of baseball's established stars. An all-out bidding war ensued, as players signed lucrative AL deals, re-signed with their NL clubs for more money, then signed with completely different AL clubs for even more.

The big winner in this battle was the American League, which opened its pocketbook in 1901 and 1902 and gained instant credibility with the signings of Young, Keeler, Delehanty, and Burkett. Many other NL regulars jumped, too, including Donlin, Griffith, Jones, Cross, and Bradley. Of the National League franchises that suffered major losses, the Boston Beaneaters got the worst of it. The team had its heart ripped out, losing Collins, Stahl, Dineen, and Freeman to the crosstown Boston Pilgrims. The AL developed some of its own stars, too.

Most notable were Socks Seybold, whose slugging feats made up for his occasional misadventures with fly balls, and lefthander Eddie Plank, a college graduate whose pinpoint control made him one of the top winners in baseball history.

Both Seybold and Plank were discovered by Connie Mack of the new Philadelphia Athletics. Mack had been angling to own a major-league team since 1890, when he jumped from the Washington Nationals to the Buffalo Bisons of the Players League. He sank his life savings of $500 into the club and lost it all when the league folded, but he did not lose his taste for being the boss. Mack worked his way back toward an ownership position by managing the Pittsburgh Pirates, then moving to the Milwaukee Brewers of the Western League, where he also ran the ballclub's business affairs. When Ban Johnson wanted someone to set up and run the American League's new Philadelphia franchise in 1901, he introduced Mack to investor Ben Shibe, who gave him a piece of the team.

One of Mack's first moves after being installed in Philadelphia was to go after the best player in town: Nap Lajoie of the Phillies. Lajoie, a big, hard-hitting second baseman, had joined fellow superstar Ed Delehanty in a celebrated holdout the season before. The two sluggers agreed that neither would play unless each received a $3,000 salary. The team offered the maximum $2,400 but promised extra money as "captain's pay." Delehanty got his $3,000, but Lajoie signed for $2,600, believing that is what his teammate had settled for. When he discovered the discrepancy, he demanded the remaining $400, but the club refused. Lajoie's frustration never subsided, eventually erupting in a clubhouse brawl

ALL·TIME Greats

HONUS WAGNER

1973 TCMA. Ltd.

Honus Wagner was Pittsburgh's star shortstop from 1900 to 1916, and he remained with the Pirates organization until 1951.

that effectively knocked the Phillies out of the 1900 pennant race. Mack knew of Lajoie's discontent, and during the winter he sent word to the angry young star through a sportswriter that he could expect at least $4,000 a year if he jumped to the Athletics. Lajoie gave the Phillies one last chance to make good on his $400 in February of 1901, but again the team refused. He signed with Mack on Valentine's Day. A lengthy court battle ensued, with the Phillies claiming the reserve clause in Lajoie's contract should prevent him from playing for the Athletics. The judge ruled against the Phillies, making Lajoie an American Leaguer. He responded by winning the triple crown, batting .422

(still an American League record) with 14 homers and 125 RBIs. Lajoie also led the junior circuit in hits, runs, total bases, on-base percentage, and slugging.

The National League still had plenty of talent, of course. In 1901 Pittsburgh took the flag with a brilliant season from Honus Wagner, who managed to lead the league in doubles, stolen bases, and RBIs while learning to play shortstop. Wagner had been wooed by Washington of the American League but swore his allegiance to Pittsburgh owner Barney Dreyfuss by signing a blank contract and telling him he could fill in any amount. The franchise rewarded his loyalty by employing him for the next 50 years. Another young player who stayed in the NL was a 20-year-old righthander who had actually signed a contract to play for Connie Mack but then backed out so he could stay with the Giants. Mack liked college men, and this particular player had graduated from Bucknell, but he had gone 0–3 in 1900 with 20 walks in 33 innings, so Mack just let the matter drop. He should have fought a little harder: Christy Mathewson won 20 games for the Giants in 1901 and would win 353 more before he retired.

Off the field, the 1902 season was even crazier than the previous year, as bidding for top players went through the roof and the tactics the leagues used on each other were getting dirtier and dirtier. It soon became obvious that the American League was perfectly capable of fighting and winning a prolonged war. Peace was declared in January 1903, with the leagues agreeing on territorial rights, ownership of disputed players, and respect for each other's contracts. They also signed a new National Agreement, which called for a three-man National Commission to oversee the game.

The end result of the two-year war was a rock-solid foundation for the national pastime and the end to three decades of instability in professional baseball. Indeed, it would be 50 years before a team so much as moved to another city and 70 years before the two leagues differed in any significant way on playing rules.

Dead Ball Days

A major reason for the early success of the American League was that Ban Johnson let it be known he would not stand for the kind of antics made popular during the 1890s by the Orioles. The fans showed their support for this cleaner style of play at the turnstiles, forcing National League owners to adopt a similar get-tough policy with their players and managers. But the most noticeable change as the 1903 season began was that baseball was fast becoming a pitcher's game. Thanks to the new rule counting foul balls as strikes (the NL had actually introduced it in 1901), hurlers could bear down on batters as never before, and batters had far fewer pitches from which to choose before picking one they liked. Batting averages plummeted and strikeouts soared. The bunt, hit-and-run, and stolen base became more important than ever.

Yet despite the lack of scoring, business boomed. Fans learned to appreciate clean, quick games that were hotly contested and crisply played. The drama of the pitcher's duel took hold of the public's imagination and also served to highlight the batting feats of the game's few offensive superstars. Defense, managing strategy, and daring baserunning became national obsessions. More and more people wanted to see major leaguers play, and toward the end of the

Opened in 1909, Shibe Park in Philadelphia was baseball's first modern stadium.

decade the owners decided it was time to spend some of the money they were making on something a little nicer than rickety wooden ballparks. In 1909, Ben Shibe built baseball's first concrete and steel stadium in Philadelphia, and 10 weeks later Barney Dreyfuss opened Forbes Field in Pittsburgh. By the end of the 1910s, every major-league team would be playing in a modern ballpark.

The period following the peace agreement produced some of the most wondrous pitchers in history. With few rules limiting what they could do to the ball and almost no chance of a batter knocking one out of the park, hurlers dominated the hitters of the day. In the American League, ex-Pirate Jack Chesbro made the New York Highlanders perennial contenders. He was one of the first pitchers to control the spitball, which darted erratically as it approached home plate. Chesbro won 41 games in 1904 but blew the pennant on the final day of the season when a wet one eluded his catcher with

the winning run on third. Ed Walsh of the White Sox actually perfected this tricky pitch. From 1906 to 1912 he was nearly untouchable, recording ERAs between 1.42 and 2.22 and setting a modern record for innings pitched in a season (464) that may never be broken. Walsh and his dipping, darting out-pitch proved ideal as an emergency reliever, and he regularly nailed down precious wins for the light-hitting Sox. The dominant role of pitching was never clearer than during the 1906 World Series, when Walsh's White Sox—nicknamed the "Hitless Wonders"—completely shut down the Chicago Cubs, who owned baseball's most powerful offense. Of the less exotic American League hurlers, Addie Joss of the Cleveland Naps was among the most effective. At 6' 3", he was tall for the time and came right at hitters with a live fastball and a tight, hard-breaking curve. Joss led the league with 27 victories in 1907, but his most remarkable year was 1908, when he limited batters to a .197 average and led the

THE WORLD SERIES RETURNS

A major factor in baseball's explosive popularity during the early part of the 20th century was the return of the World Series. It had been more than a decade since the National League and American Association champs had squared off in post-season play, and in the interim fans had only the Temple Cup (played between the NL's top two clubs), which even the players found a bit boring. In 1903, the Pittsburgh Pirates and Boston Pilgrims met to decide baseball's world championship. The best-of-nine series drew record crowds and captivated the nation's fans. In 1904, the Giants and Pilgrims won their respective pennants, but McGraw refused to let his team participate. After that the two leagues made the World Series official.

league with a microscopic 1.16 ERA. A supreme pressure pitcher, he took the mound on October 2 of that year for the biggest game of his career. Cleveland, Chicago, and Detroit were going down to the wire, and the Naps needed a win against Walsh, who had already notched 40 wins. Walsh fanned 15 hitters and allowed just one run, but Joss was even better, retiring every man he faced to record a perfect game.

Connie Mack had perhaps the best staff in the American League, with Eddie Plank good for 15 to 25 wins a year and Charley "Chief" Bender adding 15 to 20. Bender was baseball's top player of Native American descent. His father was a German immigrant and his mother was a full-blooded Chippewa. Mack's wild card, however, was Rube Waddell, a legendary screwball who was known to chase passing fire engines during games. When the Pirates and Cubs gave up on him after the 1901 season, Mack signed him for a few dollars, and Waddell

responded by delivering the 1902 pennant to the A's with 24 victories and 210 strikeouts. That started a string of six seasons in which Waddell led the majors in strikeouts. Most pitchers of the time threw the ball at 80 percent of full strength; they would hold back until they really needed a strikeout, then rear back and give it everything they had. But Waddell was not like any other pitcher. Throwing each pitch as if it were his last, he simply overpowered hitters. In 1904 he fanned 349 batters to set a league record for lefties that has yet to be broken. Mack rode Rube's arm to pennants in 1902 and 1905 but eventually tired of his antics and packed him off to St. Louis.

Christy Mathewson was the most admired, and probably the best, pitcher of his time. Handsome, intelligent, and an outspoken proponent of sportsmanship and clean play, the powerful righthander could also get down and dirty when a game was on the line. This quality probably prevented Matty and McGraw from hating each other, for on the surface there could not have been two more contradictory personalities. Mathewson's specialty was the fadeaway, a pitch that looked as if it would cut the plate in two before swerving out of the strike zone. He won 94 games between 1903 and 1905 and twirled three shutouts against the Athletics in the 1905 World Series. His rival for pitching supremacy in the National League was Mordecai Brown of the Chicago Cubs, who got his right hand caught in a corn grinder as a boy and lost parts of his index and little fingers. Holding the ball with his thumb, fourth finger and crooked middle finger, he could impart bizarre spins on his pitches. He topped 20 wins six years in a row and was the Cubs ace when they won the National League pennant each year from 1906 to 1908. Brown and Mathewson faced each other 25 times during their careers, with Matty winning 13 times. But Brown won nine in a row at one point, with the final victory coming in the playoff game that decided the 1908 pennant.

Besides Brown, Chicago had Ed Reulbach, who led the National League in winning percentage three straight times and in 1908 became the only man in history to hurl shutouts in both ends of a doubleheader. In the infield, the Cubs hurlers were backed up by Johnny Evers, Joe Tinker, Frank Chance, and Harry Steinfeldt. Chance was Chicago's first baseman and although his prime years were relatively few, he ranked among the best players of his day and was also an excellent manager. Tinker was a superb defensive shortstop who handled the bat well and was a very good baserunner. Steinfeldt, who had been with the Cubs for a decade, provided clutch hitting and sure hands at third. Evers, though, was the heart of the Cubs. He weighed just 125 pounds,

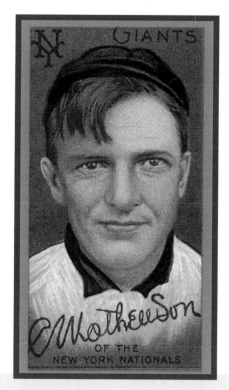

Christy Mathewson was the most admired pitcher of the Dead Ball era.

yet he was considered one of the most dangerous offensive players in the league. A brilliant situational hitter and the epitome of a head's-up defensive player, Evers was perhaps the most valuable sparkplug in the game. Steady Johnny Kling was behind the plate, and the outfield featured Jimmy Slagle, Jimmy Sheckard, and Wildfire Schulte. Sheckard was a terrific leftfielder with plenty of pop in his bat, while Schulte had a cannon arm in right. In center, the speedy Slagle was nicknamed the "Human Mosquito" for the way he buzzed around the bases. Needless to say, this Cubs team was one of the greatest in history.

Toward the end of the decade, the Detroit Tigers moved to the top of the American League. Detroit had struggled during its

The famed infield of (left to right) third baseman Harry Steinfeldt, shortstop Joe Tinker, second baseman Johnny Evers, and Frank Chance—led the Cubs to four pennants in five years.

first few years in the AL but began its climb toward respectability after acquiring the game's top young slugger, Sam Crawford, and George Mullin, a power pitcher signed out of the semipro ranks. The final piece of the puzzle was Ty Cobb, a troubled young man from rural Georgia who seemed incapable of having a civilized relationship with anybody. When Cobb joined the Tigers as an 18-year-old rookie at the end of the 1906 season, the veterans gave him a rough time. This was, and still is, one of baseball's rituals—a little teasing, a practical joke, the silent treatment—but Cobb did not understand that this is the way major leaguers welcome new guys to the team. He offered to fight them all. When they declined, he decided to hate them all. Cobb was haunted by some very personal demons, but he managed to channel his paranoia and rage into his baseball. Within a year he was the most relentless offensive player in the game, and the Tigers vaulted from sixth place to the top of the league. It

was the first of three consecutive pennants for Detroit.

Alex the Great and the Big Train

As the second decade of the 20th century began, the old guard of pitching was being replaced by young hurlers who understood what it took to win: a little speed, an occasional pinch of deception, and, most important, pinpoint control. The player who best embodied these qualities was Grover Cleveland Alexander. As a 24-year-old rookie in 1911, "Alex the Great" won 28 games for the Phillies and twirled four consecutive shutouts along the way. In 1915, he pitched the franchise to its first pennant, winning 31 times, striking out 241, and posting a 1.22 ERA. Alexander threw a fastball that bent downward as it approached the plate, causing batters to bang it into the ground. He could change speeds on this pitch and occasionally mixed in a curveball. Extra-base

FEDERAL LEAGUE

In the spring of 1913, a group of baseball-loving midwestern businessmen got together and formed their own professional baseball league. The Federal League made no claims of being on a par with the American and National Leagues. It hired former big leaguers to manage its six teams but stocked its rosters with minor leaguers, semipro players, and others on the fringes of baseball. The Feds gave the fans decent baseball at a fair price.

Then, in 1914, the Federal League got aggressive. It expanded to eight teams, placed franchises in several eastern cities, and began offering established AL and NL stars high salaries to break their contracts. Joe Tinker and Mordecai Brown of the Cubs switched leagues, as did several other stars. Many who stayed with their teams used the Federal League to negotiate better salaries. After one season of direct competition, the Feds were thriving. A close pennant race had kept attendance high, and they had been able to fend off a series of lawsuits brought by the AL and NL that were aimed at draining the Federal League's finances.

In January 1915, the Federal League sued the two established leagues, claiming they had an illegal monopoly on players thanks to the reserve clause. The Feds chose to enter their case before Judge Kenesaw Mountain Landis, who had a reputation for being tough on monopolies. But Landis saw baseball as being different from an ordinary business and put off a decision until after the 1915 season. By then, a peace agreement was drawn up, and the lawsuits were dropped. The Federal League was disbanded, its stars returned, and a "reparations" payment was made to the owners of the failed circuit by the NL and AL. Two of the Federal League owners, Phil Ball and Charlie Weeghman, wanted to stay in the game, and they purchased the Indians and Cubs, respectively.

hits were rare when he had his good stuff; the best a hitter could hope for was to get good wood on the ball and pray it found its way between two infielders. What separated Alexander from the other control pitchers of his era was that he could throw hard enough to win when his out-pitch was not working. Most hurlers of the time banked on upsetting a hitter's timing by changing speeds and locations, but as a rule they did not possess overpowering stuff. As a result, there were precious few who managed to put up great numbers for more than two or three years in a row.

Fastball pitchers, however, fared no better. In an era in which training and playing conditions were still primitive by present standards, hard throwers typically chalked

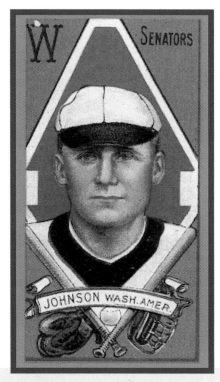

Walter Johnson was baseball's hardest-throwing pitcher for two decades.

up one or two good years before hurting their arms. And with sports medicine being equally primitive, there was little chance of their recovering. Only one fastball specialist pitched at a consistently high level throughout the decade—Walter Johnson. He joined the Washington starting rotation in 1908, and by 1910 he had harnessed his smooth, sidearm delivery and began whipping the ball past hitters at more than 95 miles per hour. Johnson led the American League with 313 strikeouts at the tender age of 22 and continued to overpower enemies well into his 30s. From 1910 to 1919, he led the league in strikeouts nine times and averaged 26 wins per season. A gentle, gracious man who lived in fear of what his fastball might do if it hit an opponent in the head (batting

helmets were still decades away), Johnson rarely pitched hitters inside. Yet despite the fact that enemy batters could dig in and take their best cuts against "The Big Train," Johnson's ERA climbed above 2.00 only once during the entire decade.

A Whole New Ball

Ben Shibe, who gave baseball its first modern ballpark, also gave the game its first modern ball. In 1909, he invented a cork-center baseball that proved so popular both leagues decided to use it for the 1911 season. It had the same weight and feel as the old ball, which had a rubber center, but held its shape better and longer. It also had a lot more life to it. Batting averages soared in 1911 and 1912, and the fans seemed to love it. After growing steadily during the early 1900s, major-league attendance had topped out at 7.2 million in 1909, and the owners could not figure out why. They were building new ballparks, and there were plenty of new pitching stars—what could possibly be the matter? They may have had their answer during 1911, only it seems they did not realize it at the time. During that season attendance jumped more than 6 percent. When the owners started tinkering with the ball again, causing a drop-off in hitting, attendance plunged to its lowest level since 1902.

The fans were apparently tiring of stingy pitching. Now they wanted lusty hitting. And there were a number of players around who could provide it. In the AL, Ty Cobb remained the most feared hitter, but close behind him were Joe Jackson and Tris Speaker. Jackson hit for a high average and possessed tremendous power at a time when batting averages were low and most players were happy with singles. He was discovered in the back woods of South Carolina by Connie Mack and brought to Philadelphia, where the team's veterans teased him unmercifully. Jackson could barely read and write, spoke with a heavy drawl, and was totally unprepared for life as a major leaguer. He withdrew from his fellow players and failed to produce, so Mack shipped him to Cleveland. There, he blossomed into a devastating offensive force, leading the league in hits twice before he was traded to the White Sox. Jackson continued his brilliant play in the Windy City, helping the team win pennants in 1917 and 1919. Speaker was the game's premiere defensive outfielder and the hitting star of the pen-

nant-winning Red Sox teams in 1912 and 1915. He played a shallow centerfield, which enabled him to catch many of the balls that would have fallen for singles in right- and left-center. He could also go back on the ball as well as anyone who ever played. Speaker was the man most often compared to Cobb during the 1910s, and many felt he was a better all-around player. He was faster in the field and on the basepaths than the Detroit star and hit for a bit more power. Speaker also boasted a better arm and was clearly better getting to the ball in the outfield.

Despite getting nothing in return for Joe Jackson, the Philadelphia Athletics won the American League pennant four times be-

WORLD WAR I

Although the United States entered the Great War in 1917, it was not until the 1918 season that baseball was affected. Because the game was deemed "non-essential" to the war effort, players technically had to enlist in the military or work at jobs that supported the war effort. Luckily, Secretary of War Baker granted baseball a grace period, so that the game could continue. The schedule was reduced to 128 games, with the season ending on September 2, but the World Series went on as planned. Many major leaguers were drafted that year, and many more enlisted. Those who stayed and played sometimes put on marching exhibitions prior to games, carrying bats on their shoulders instead of rifles.

Fans also became familiar with a song that would one day become a baseball tradition: "The Star Spangled Banner." There were two notable casualties of World War I. Eddie Grant, a graduate of Harvard, had been a top third baseman for the Giants before retiring to practice law in 1915. He was cut down by machine gun fire leading a daring rescue mission behind German lines. Christy Mathewson, who had retired to manage the Reds in 1916, enlisted as an Army captain in 1918 and was exposed to poison gas during a training exercise. He contracted tuberculosis as a result and died a few years later at the age of 47.

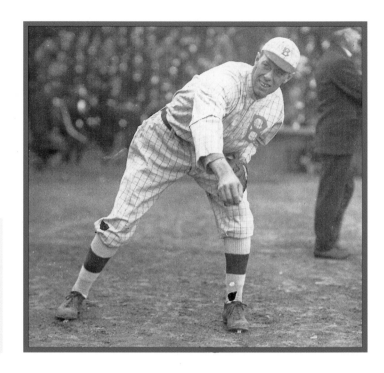

Brooklyn pitcher Jack Coombs sports one of the strangest uniforms in major-league history. It proved to be good luck, as the team won the pennant in 1916.

tween 1910 and 1914. They did it with solid pitching and airtight interior defense supplied by Mack's "$100,000 Infield." Two members of that infield, Eddie Collins and Frank "Home Run" Baker, also paced the team's offense. Collins was the best all-around second baseman of his day, and possibly of all time. Splitting the decade with the Athletics and the White Sox, he led his team to the pennant on six occasions with near-flawless fielding, blazing speed on the bases, and consistent excellence at the plate. Baker, who played third base, was one of the game's rare sluggers. He was strong enough to muscle pitches out of the park— leading the league in homers from 1911 to 1914—but he was also a solid .300 hitter.

The National League had fewer offensive superstars during this time. The great Honus Wagner was still the best shortstop in baseball, but he won just one more batting title after 1909. Ten different players led the league in hits between 1910 and 1919, and

the only repeat batting champions were Jake Daubert and Edd Roush. The league's smoothest swing belonged to Zach Wheat. The Brooklyn outfielder was a line-drive machine who feasted on the off-speed pitching that was so prevalent during the decade. He played leftfield and batted cleanup for the club for 17 seasons. Heinie Zimmerman, a sub for the Cubs during their pennant years, took over at third base in 1912 and quickly established himself as one of the game's top power hitters. A 1916 trade sent him to the Giants, where he became the team's best man in the clutch, leading them to the 1917 pennant.

The concepts of hard throwing and heavy hitting never really took hold during the second decade of the 20th century. Baseball had been a game of finesse and strategy for so long that virtually every player who made it to the majors had been schooled in this approach from the first day he picked up a ball. Runs were something hitters had to scratch and claw for; outs were earned by pitchers who made the ball dance through the strike zone at speeds just tempting enough to induce ill-advised swings. This did not apply to a rawboned pitcher named George "Babe" Ruth, who joined the Boston Red Sox for a few games in July of 1914. He was 19 years old, and the only things he had been schooled in were cursing, spitting, fighting, stealing, and otherwise living life at the extremes. No one had taught George the "right" way to play baseball when he was in reform school, and now that he was out in the world with some money in his pocket, no one was going to tell him anything.

There was little science to the way Ruth worked hitters—he kept it low, kept it fast, and just let the ball's natural movement do the rest. And there was no science at all to the way he hit. Ruth waited menacingly for the pitcher to go through his windup and then whipped his bat around with everything he had. He struck out a lot, but when he connected the ball came off his bat with a sound that gave a pitcher chills. During the 1915 season he batted in 42 games—10 as a pinch-hitter—and crashed four home runs, 10 doubles and had the highest slugging average on the team by more than 150 points. What caught everyone by surprise, however, was not that Ruth went about playing baseball totally oblivious to the conventions of the day. It was the reaction he elicited from the fans wherever he appeared. For some strange reason, they seemed to adore him.

Over the next two seasons, Ruth established himself as the finest left-hander in baseball, winning 47 games, recording 15 shutouts and leading the league in 1916 with a 1.75 ERA. Still, it was his remark-

able hitting that brought the Fenway Park crowd to its feet. In 1918, the Red Sox began playing Ruth in leftfield and reduced his pitching starts from 38 to 19. He responded with 13 victories and also led the American League in home runs and slugging average. In 1919, as a full-time offensive player, he set the modern record for home runs in a season with 29 and led the league in runs scored, RBIs, and slugging. Ruth blatantly ignored the common wisdom of baseball, playing instead the way he wanted to play. It made no sense to him to bunt and steal and hit-and-run. Why not just clobber the ball and trot around the bases? Soon, all of baseball would come around to Ruth's way of thinking.

Rule Changes

The owners had big plans for baseball as the 1920 season approached. In an attempt to increase scoring, they banned spitballs and other doctored pitches, finally tilting the advantage back toward the hitters. The major leagues also began using a slightly different ball. It was the same basic cork-center model used since 1911, but the yarn that was wrapped around it was of better quality and was probably wrapped a little tighter. The idea was to create a game with a little more offense in order to reverse the lackluster attendance figures that had plagued baseball for an entire decade. These changes, however, did not intrigue fans nearly as much as the fact that the 1920 season would find Babe Ruth in the league's most populous market, New York City. Boston Red Sox owner Harry Frazee had made his fortune producing plays, and in order to finance his new project, *No! No! Nanette!*, he needed to raise a lot of cash.

BABE RUTH
NEW YORK AMERICANS

THE BAMBINO

George Ruth spent his childhood in Baltimore bouncing back and forth between his family's seedy waterfront saloon and the St. Mary's Industrial School for Boys, which was little more than a prison for children. The main focus of life at St. Mary's was baseball and discipline. Ruth was a natural when it came to throwing, hitting, running, and catching. Nothing had to be explained to him; he just understood how the game was played. This was not true, however, when it came to discipline. Although he spent most of his young life in a reform school, he just did not get what it was all about. Ruth was not much on rules, and his first instinct when pushed was to push back. He had a difficult time concentrating and threw tantrums whenever things did not go his way. He could barely read or write and had trouble uttering a complete sentence without injecting a curse or two.

Ruth's big chance was baseball, and everyone at St. Mary's knew it. A lot of good ballplayers had passed through there, including a few future major leaguers, but this boy was something special. He was huge yet graceful; his reflexes were quick, and his instincts were impeccable. When he hit the ball, it traveled so far so fast that it seemed to defy the laws of physics; when he threw it, it cut through the air like a rifle shot. At first, Ruth was a catcher, but around the age of 16 or 17, he moved to the mound, where he enjoyed instant success. He threw harder than most major leaguers, probably over 90 miles per hour.

In 1913, when Ruth was 18, Joe Engel of the Washington Senators saw him pitch against another reform school and tipped off Jack Dunn, the owner of the Baltimore Orioles. The Orioles were a well-known minor league team that had set up shop back in 1903 when the American League Orioles moved to New York. Dunn, who had also received a letter from St. Mary's about the boy, decided to scout Ruth himself. He was always on the lookout for young talent. Ticket sales barely covered operating expenses for the team, so to turn a profit Dunn developed players to the point where they were ready for the major leagues and then offered them to the highest bidder. Dunn asked for a game to be arranged between St. Mary's and Mount St. Joseph, an exclusive Catholic school, which had another pitcher he wished to scout, named Bill Morrisette. Ruth was magnificent, striking out 14 and winning 8-0. He also exhibited a real talent for working the crowd. That was all

Dunn needed to see. He arranged to become the boy's guardian and checked him out of St. Mary's in time for spring training in 1914.

Ruth, of course, worked out just fine. He had no trouble retiring hitters in the International League, and he struck out Frank Baker and Eddie Collins during an exhibition game with the Athletics. Dunn was so pleased he tore up Ruth's initial contract and tripled his salary. His teammates found their young star charming in his own crude way and welcomed him to the team with his very own nickname. They called him "Dunn's Babe," or just plain "Babe." Despite the spirited start, the 1914 season was not a good one for the Orioles. The Federal League had placed a franchise in Baltimore and stocked it with a couple of big-time pitchers, Jack Quinn and George Suggs, as well as Otto Knabe and Mickey Doolan, the Phillies double-play combination from the year before. Baltimore fans began splitting their loyalties—especially when such big stars as Joe Tinker, Chief Bender, Mordecai Brown, and George Mullin came to town—and Dunn was getting murdered at the turnstiles. He hated to do it, but he had no choice; it was time to sell the Babe.

Connie Mack had expressed interest back in March when Ruth fanned his two best hitters, but the Federal League franchise in Philadelphia was killing him, too. He hated to let the boy slip through his fingers, but he could not spare the cash. Red Sox owner Joe Lannin, hearing of Dunn's predicament, offered $8,900, but he demanded Baltimore's three best prospects: Ruth, catcher Ben Egan, and pitcher Ernie Shore. Dunn reluctantly accepted and moved his club to Richmond, Virginia, until the Feds left town a year later. Ruth, who had been in reform school just a few months earlier, was now a major-league pitcher for the Boston Red Sox.

Manager Bill Carrigan handed the ball to his new pitcher a day after he arrived and told him to show him what he had. The Cleveland Indians were in town, led by Joe Jackson and Napolean Lajoie. That did not rattle Ruth; he had never heard of them. He went seven innings and won. A couple of days later, Shore got his chance. He pitched well, too. Carrigan, only able to carry one rookie hurler, chose Shore. He called Ruth into his office, handed him a train ticket and told him he was headed for the minors. Carrigan promised he would get a shot at the starting rotation the following spring. Carrigan stuck to his word, and Ruth made him happy he did by winning 18 games and helping the Red Sox win the 1915 pennant. The Babe was in the majors to stay.

Frazee sold the Babe to the Yankees for $100,000 (more than three times the previous record) and also obtained a $300,000 loan from the team.

As the season wore on, it became apparent that the rule changes were working. Scoring was up, although not as dramatically as in 1911. The big difference was Ruth, who had the kind of season once thought impossible. Playing in 142 games, the 25-year-old slugger hit 54 homers, knocked in 137 runs and scored 158. His slugging average was an eye-popping .847, and he reached base more than half the time he came to the plate. So completely did Ruth destroy American League pitching that by mid-summer there was talk of curbing the offensive explosion before it "ruined" baseball.

In August, Ruth's teammate, Carl Mays, hit Cleveland shortstop Ray Chapman in the head with one of his strange, submarine-style deliveries. Chapman, an immensely popular player around the league, lost track of the pitch and froze; the ball struck him flush in the temple, and he died from his injuries. It was the first time a major leaguer had been killed on the field, and a good part of the blame lay with the policy of allowing a ball to stay in play until it was either lost or damaged. The ball that beaned Chapman was not shiny and white like today's baseballs but a dirty brownish-gray sphere discolored by dirt and tobacco juice. Pitchers hated new balls because hitters could see and hit them better. Whenever a new ball was put into play a pitcher would whip it around the infield so his teammates could camouflage it with various foreign substances.

The Chapman beaning was a huge blow to baseball. But what happened on September 28 was nothing short of a catastrophe. Acting upon rumors that had been circulating since the previous fall, a Chicago grand jury found enough evidence to indict eight White Sox players on charges that they conspired to lose the 1919 World Series. An elaborate plot hatched by a professional gambler named Arnold Rothstein was to pay Joe Jackson and other key players $100,000 to throw the series to the Cincinnati Reds, who were heavy underdogs. Chicago owner Charlie Comiskey immediately suspended the players in question, fielding a skeleton team for the season's final two weeks. The Indians, behind player-manager Tris Speaker's magnificent leadership and the fine play of Chapman's replacement, Joe Sewell, rallied down the stretch to edge Chicago and New York for the pennant.

The hitting revolution that began in 1920 had less to do with lively baseballs than it did with the dynamic events of that season. The owners were terrified of what the "Black Sox" scandal would do to their game, especially after a year in which attendance had jumped by almost 50 percent. What if fans, disillusioned by the specter of game-fixing (and horrified at the thought of witnessing another death) simply decided to stay away? The owners did the smart thing. They crossed their fingers, and for the first time in a long time, let the game go its own way.

The Roaring Twenties

Between the 1920 and 1921 seasons, some important changes took place. First, the owners got rid of the three-man National Commission they had created in 1903 and replaced it with the office of baseball commissioner. The post would carry with it absolute power over all matters in baseball—a necessary measure to restore the public trust. They gave the job to Kenesaw Mountain Landis, the federal judge who had impressed the owners with his handling of the antitrust suit brought against them by the Federal League. Landis immediately issued lifetime suspensions to 15 ballplayers for their part in the Black Sox scandal. The second important change prior to the 1921 season addressed the Chapman tragedy. The umpires were instructed to keep a clean ball in the game at all times. If a ball needed "rubbing up" to give it a better grip, that would be the responsibility of the umps, not the pitchers. The third and final change in baseball came in the collective mindset of the game's hitters. Babe Ruth destroyed supposedly unhittable pitching by going up to the plate, waiting for a good one, and then letting it rip. He was rich, famous, and popular, and in one season he broke more than a dozen batting records. The heck with the old style, many players decided, we are going to do it the Babe's way!

So in 1921, a lot of players were swinging harder at balls they could see better, being delivered by pitchers who were not allowed to doctor them up. Consequently, scoring was up nearly a run per game in the American League, and batting averages rose by eight points. In the National League the difference was far more dramatic, as scoring was up by more than a run per contest and batting averages skyrocketed from .270 to .289. As for Ruth, he actually managed to improve on his 1920 campaign. He broke his own home-run record with 59, scored 177 runs, and drove in 171. More important, he led the Yankees to their first

pennant in franchise history. As for the huge drop in attendance the owners feared, it never materialized. There was a small backlash by the fans over the "Black Sox" scandal, but the actual decline was no more than 6 or 7 percent.

Although most of the power hitting was being done in the American League during the 1920s, it was the National League that produced the first great offensive team of the decade. The New York Giants, who won the pennant each year from 1921 to 1924, were built around a consistent and well-rounded attack that featured a little of everything, from power to speed to clutch hitting. The heart of the team was second baseman Frankie Frisch, a brilliant on-field leader who blended old-time base stealing with a potent bat. While Frisch tore up the basepaths, George "Highpockets" Kelly was the team's major home-run threat, hitting between 16 and 23 homers a season during New York's big years and claiming a couple of RBI titles in the process.

Frisch remained with the Giants through the 1926 season, when he was traded even-up to St. Louis for second baseman Rogers Hornsby, the most productive right-handed hitter in history. Hornsby had broken in with the Cardinals during the 1910s and hit reasonably well. But in 1920 he had a breakout season, winning his first of six straight batting titles with a .370 average. From there, "Rajah" just got better. His average kept climbing until it reached a high of .424 in 1924, and he continued to pound the ball at an unprecedented clip for another five years. From 1920 to 1925, there was not a better offensive performer in the National League. No one was even close. As one might imagine, Hornsby took his hitting seriously. He rarely read and

Satchel Paige's 1948 autobiography attests to his immense popularity.

THE NEGRO LEAGUES

During the 1920s, the first truly organized professional league for African-American ballplayers was formed. The idea was nothing new—the all-black Cuban Giants had been formed way back in 1885—but it took the skill and foresight of pitcher-manager-entrepreneur Rube Foster to turn black baseball from a collection of barnstorming outfits into a true league. For a decade he guided the Negro National League, which was centered in the midwest. The Eastern Colored League was formed as a rival circuit in 1923, bringing together teams from the East Coast, and a "World Series" was played from 1924 to 1927. Both leagues disbanded shortly thereafter, and during the Great Depression several attempts were made to restart organized leagues.

Most teams simply continued operating as best they could, and that meant traveling by bus and car from town to town, playing local teams and occasionally meeting each other. The highlight of black baseball during the Depression was the East-West All-Star Game, which showcased such offensive stars as sluggers Josh Gibson and Buck Leonard, Ray Dandridge and Judy Johnson (the two best third basemen—black or white—in history to that time), shortstop Willie Wells, Martin Dihigo, who was a world-class fielder at five different positions, and Cool Papa Bell, who might have been the fastest man ever to play professional ball. Among the standout pitchers of the 1920s and 1930s were Willie Foster (Rube's younger half-brother), fireballer Leon Day, and the most celebrated African-American player of his time, Satchel Paige. These players took over the spotlight from early stars, such as centerfielder Oscar Charleston and shortstop John Henry Lloyd, whom Honus Wagner felt was every bit his equal in the field and at the plate.

Few records were kept from this important part of professional baseball, and the ones that do exist are not very reliable. But from newspaper accounts and from the major leaguers who often played against them in post-season games, it is quite clear that the top players of black baseball during the first half of the 20th century were just as good—and possibly even better—than the top players in the big leagues. It is almost impossible to imagine how good major-league baseball might have been during the 16-team era had African-Americans been allowed to play.

never went to the movies; he did not smoke cigarettes, nor did he drink alcohol or coffee. After a year in New York, Hornsby was dealt to the Boston Braves, who then shipped him to the Cubs for $200,000 and five players. The huge price tag was worth it, as he led the league in slugging for the ninth time, nearly won the Triple Crown, and got Chicago back into the World Series for the first time since the days of Tinker, Evers, and Chance. Babe Ruth may have hit for more power, and Ty Cobb may have edged him in the batting average department, but no one ever combined both schools of hitting as well as Hornsby.

In the American League, the Yankees dominated for most of the decade, winning pennants from 1921 to 1923 and 1926 to 1928. Besides Ruth, New York had two other players who played prominent roles in all six championships, pitcher Waite Hoyt and leftfielder Bob Meusel. Hoyt came from the Red Sox a year after Ruth and won 55 games over the next three seasons. He did not have overpowering stuff, but his control was good enough to make batters swing at his pitch, and he was content to let his fielders record the outs. During the team's three pennants in the late 1920s, Hoyt had all but mastered his craft, averaging better than 20 wins a season. Meusel was an aggressive, ill-tempered star who had little interest in anything other than winning ballgames and cashing World Series checks. Still, he was one of the game's most complete players. Meusel could hit for average and power, run the bases, catch anything hit his way, and he had a cannon for an arm.

Meusel batted fourth, behind Ruth, through the 1926 season. He dropped down to fifth in the order when the Yankees found an even better cleanup hitter in first baseman Lou Gehrig. He became a regular in 1925, but not until 1927 did he emerge as a serious home-run threat. A massively built left-hander who hit the ball even harder than Ruth, Gehrig was the boisterous Babe's complete opposite in terms of demeanor. This led to an uneasy relationship between the two men, and for several years they did not speak. As a one-two punch, however, they were the best ever. From 1927—when Ruth broke his own record with 60 homers and Gehrig chipped in 47—through 1934, the duo combined for 663 round-trippers, or

PEACH OF A PLAYER

By the 1920s, Ty Cobb's string of batting titles had come to an end, but he still hit in the high .300s until he retired in 1928. Cobb hated the new obsession with power hitting, feeling the game had passed him by. He despised Ruth and was often quoted that it took no talent to hit home runs. After a while, reporters stopped listening to his griping, which infuriated him even more. One day, before a game against the Browns, he told reporters he would show them how easy it was to hit home runs—and proceeded to deposit three balls into the bleachers!

Lou Gehrig emerged from Ruth's shadow to become a Yankees legend.

roughly three every five games. Gehrig's presence in the lineup enabled Ruth to see good pitches well into his twilight years, for pitchers did not want to put a man on base with "Larrupin' Lou" coming up next. And with Ruth hitting .300 in front of him, Gehrig was constantly up with a man on base. The result was that Ruth was the American League's perennial home run champ, while Gehrig won the RBI crown five times in eight years. He also averaged more RBIs per home run than anyone in history.

The 1927 edition of the New York Yankees featured these players, along with an excellent supporting cast. Setting the table for "Murderers Row" was Earle Combs. He led the American League in putouts, hits, and triples that year, which is about all anyone could ask from a man who played cen-

Many baseball historians consider the 1927 Yankees the best baseball team ever.

terfield and batted leadoff. Bringing up the rear of the order was second baseman Tony Lazzeri, who socked 18 homers and drove home 102 runs from the six-hole. The Yankee pitching staff featured Hoyt and several effective veterans, including Herb Pennock and Urban Shocker.

Although Ruth and Gehrig set the tone for home-run hitters, they were not the only big bats in the American League during the 1920s. Leftfielder Ken Williams did some serious fence busting for the St. Louis Browns, especially in 1922, when he became the first player in baseball history to hit 30 home runs, steal 30 bases, and bat .300 in the same season. The Browns missed winning the pennant by one game that year, despite an even better season from first baseman George Sisler, who batted .420 with a league-high 51 steals. Like Ruth, he began his major-league career as a left-handed pitcher, and he too was a good one. And like Ruth, Sisler was an excellent hitter even back in baseball's Dead Ball days. That, however, is where the similarities ended. Sisler was a line-drive hitter, a defensive genius, and one of the fastest players in the league. Before Gehrig came along, most people considered Sisler the best first baseman of all time, and there were some who felt that way even after Gehrig left the game.

A couple of other AL hitting stars during the 1920s were Harry Heilmann and Leon "Goose" Goslin. Heilmann had broken in with the Tigers during the 1910s but came into his own during the 1920s. The rightfielder's defense was nothing to brag about, but he more than made up for it by winning four batting titles between 1921 and 1928. Goslin played leftfield and batted cleanup for the Washington Senators, who

Tigers outfielder Harry Heilmann won four batting titles in the 1920s.

played their games in cavernous Griffith Stadium (where even the mighty Ruth had trouble reaching the fences). Had Goslin played in, say, Fenway Park, he might have hit 40 round-trippers a year. Despite this home-field disadvantage, he managed to knock in 100 runs almost annually and was good for 60 to 75 extra-base hits a season during his days as a Senator.

Still going strong in Philadelphia was Connie Mack, who rebuilt his club to suit the new style of ball played in the 1920s. He started with centerfielder Al Simmons, a man who liked to leave his mark on opponents, whether smashing a line drive off a pitcher's leg or wiping out a shortstop while breaking up a double play. The right-handed Simmons was a devastating hitter, even though his form was devastatingly bad. As the ball approached the plate, he would "pull off" it, stepping toward third base. He made up for this flaw with extra-long arms and an extra-long bat. Mack's other find was Mickey Cochrane, a catcher who handled his defensive duties with great skill and also could handle himself at the plate. Cochrane was a fiery on-field leader, and a supreme handler of pitchers. But what distinguished him from other backstops of the 1920s was his offense. Cochrane was a legitimate .300 hitter with speed and power. The Athletics challenged the Yankees for supremacy in the American League for much of the decade, but not until Mack converted Cochrane's backup, Jimmie Foxx, into a first baseman, did Philadelphia finally win a pennant.

Philadelphia's pitching star was Robert "Lefty" Grove. In an era when offense ruled, Grove was in a class by himself. A product of Jack Dunn's Baltimore Orioles, Grove actually could have been a major-league star a few years before he came to the Athletics, but Dunn refused to sell him too cheaply, as he had been forced to do with Babe Ruth. Grove spent five years with the Orioles, during which the team won the International League pennant five times. He won 27 games in each of his last two minor league seasons, bringing the bidding up over the $100,000 mark. Mack, remembering how he had missed getting Ruth for a fraction of that sum, ponied up $100,600 for Grove and he turned out to be worth every penny. Lefty threw very hard, and although he was wild at times, within a couple of seasons he had developed superb control. Then the wins just kept piling up: 20 in 1927, 24 in 1928, another 20 in 1929, and 108 more for the A's from 1930 to 1933. Grove led the AL in strikeouts in each of his first seven seasons, and regularly posted ERAs in the

2.00s when the league average was in the 4.00s. He may not have thrown as hard as Walter Johnson in his prime, but unlike Johnson, he threw inside, sawing off bats and intimidating hitters.

In the National League, the most impressive pitcher was Brooklyn's Dazzy Vance, who won the strikeout championship each year between 1922 and 1928. Vance had been a minor-league sensation during the previous decade but was plagued by control problems and a chronically tired arm. He did the unthinkable back then by undergoing surgery and also bucked convention by demanding four days' rest instead of the customary three accorded most starters at the time. The results were nothing short of amazing, as he became the league's toughest pitcher at the age of 31 and remained so for most of the 1920s.

As the decade drew to a close, there was no question which way baseball was headed. The fans were in love with high-powered offense, and they idolized the game's sluggers. Babe Ruth had shown the way, and everyone followed. In the process, Ruth became the world's first sports superstar and the highest-salaried athlete in history. His face was instantly recognizable, and his name was known throughout the world, even by people who had never witnessed a baseball game. Ruth was also baseball's savior. Had he not come along when he did, there is no telling what would have happened in the wake of the crooked 1919 World Series. As Judge Landis pressed his investigation into game-fixing beyond the Black Sox scandal, he discovered that ballplayers had been conspiring to throw games for years. By the end of the 1920s, though, the game was squeaky clean, and the indiscretions of 1919 had been forgiven

Young fans surround their hero, Babe Ruth. Ruth remained the game's most popular hero even after his retirement in 1935.

and nearly forgotten. The economy was booming, America was the greatest place in the world, and each year more than nine million people paid their way into major league ballparks to watch their heroes play.

Hard Times

The 1920s had been a time of great prosperity, both for baseball and the United States. Needless to say the two were not unrelated. Ruth and the other sluggers may have enticed fans into the ballparks, but they went in unprecedented numbers because they could afford to go and because they had the time to go. America had rebounded brilliantly from the dark years of World War I; there were more jobs, and more high-paying jobs, than at any time in history. People also had a lot more leisure time, and millions spent their free hours at NL and AL ballparks.

Throughout the decade, the stock market made many Americans rich beyond their wildest dreams. Even toward the end of the 1920s, when many economists were cautioning that the market was unreasonably high, people continued to pour their savings into stocks, and the market continued to rise. Although only a small fraction of Americans actually invested money in the market, the profits they reaped fueled the economy and positively affected millions of lives. Furthermore, Wall Street's apparent invincibility was a great comfort to people in the United States. It affirmed that the country was healthy and that prosperity would never end.

In the autumn of 1929, things started to change. The stock market finally began to fall. People who were wealthy one day were broke the next. The economy slumped and got progressively worse as the 1930s began. Eventually, it slowed to a crawl. Millions of

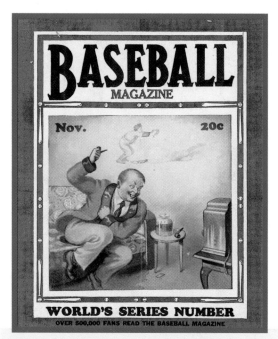

The cover of this 1931 issue of *Baseball Magazine* underscores the influence that radio broadcasts of games had on the increasing popularity of the national pastime.

people lost their jobs, and the supreme confidence that once filled the hearts and minds of America was replaced by hopelessness, bitterness, and despair. Although attendance climbed higher than ever during the 1930 season, baseball was about to face its sternest test. The Great Depression was slowly consuming the United States, and the game would suffer with it.

As America's dire situation became clear to the owners, they agreed that for baseball to be profitable it would have to provide city people with an escape from the misery surrounding them and the pressures of everyday life. This goal was greatly enhanced by radio, which kept fans connected to the game when they could not make it to the park. It gave players a bigger-than-life

quality that was crucial to positioning baseball as a special part of the American landscape. Baseball also generated fan interest by establishing an official Most Valuable Player Award (in the past, this honor had been bestowed by outside companies), an All-Star Game (in 1933), and the Hall of Fame (1936).

The decade began with a wild season, as batting averages and power hitting reached all-time highs in 1930. Hack Wilson, a fireplug-shaped outfielder for the Cubs, knocked in 190 runs and slugged 56 homers to establish National League records that stand to this day. Bill Terry, the first baseman for the New York Giants, became the last National Leaguer to bat .400 and set a league record with 254 hits. In the AL the scene was the same, with Ruth, Gehrig, Simmons, and Foxx putting up eye-popping numbers. The fans loved it, but the owners got a little scared when even last-place teams were able to produce a .300 batting average. So prior to the 1931 season, some minor adjustments were made in the manufacture of the baseball, and batting stats returned to the levels of the 1920s. For the rest of the decade, the balance between hitters and pitchers stayed more or less the same, with hitters doing a little better in the AL and pitchers having a bit more success in the NL. The dominant team was the New York Yankees, but that club did not come together until the latter half of the 1930s. Prior to that, the best all-around team was the Philadelphia Athletics, and the most interesting team was the St. Louis Cardinals.

The Athletics won the AL pennant in 1929, 1930 and 1931, as the players assembled by Connie Mack in the 1920s all matured at the same time. Grove, Simmons, and Cochrane were joined by a very capable supporting cast, which included outfielders Bing Miller and Mule Haas and infielders Jimmy Dykes and Max Bishop. Meanwhile, Grove was backed up by two more hard throwers, Rube Walberg and George Earnshaw. The key to the team was Foxx, a magnificent physical specimen with supreme offensive and defensive skills. He was nicknamed "The Beast," and a look at his statistics show why: from 1930 to 1935, the Philadelphia first sacker blasted 253 homers. In 1933, he won the Triple Crown with 48 home runs, 163 RBIs and a .356 average. Incredibly, that was not even his best year. In 1932, he hit 58 home runs, knocked in 169 runs and batted .364. Later in the 1930s, after being sold to the Red Sox, he hit 50 homers with 175 RBIs and led the league with a .349 average. For the decade, Foxx averaged 41 home runs and 140 RBIs a year.

The Gas House Gang

The team that met the Athletics in the 1930 and 1931 World Series was the St. Louis Cardinals. Clutch-hitting Jim Bottomley and Frankie Frisch were the big names on the club, along with rifle-armed leftfielder Chick Hafey and ace pitcher "Wild Bill" Hallahan, who earned his nickname with an exploding fastball that every so often exploded a foot or two out of the strike zone. The 1931 team also featured a 27-year-old rookie named Pepper Martin. Martin was short on natural ability but long on enthusiasm, and his aggressive style on the base paths often caught opponents by surprise. Much was expected of this club in the ensuing seasons, but in 1932 and 1933 a combination of age and underachievement caused the Cards to finish far off the pace. During

those years, Branch Rickey, a brilliant and innovative general manager, began developing baseball's first farm system. The Cardinals purchased teams at various levels of the minor leagues and entered into exclusive working arrangements with others so that they could control a young player's progress and get first crack at him when he was ready for the majors. This arrangement also benefited the minor league clubs, which got money, equipment, and better coaching thanks to the Cards.

By 1934, Rickey had successfully retooled the team and named Frisch as player-manager. Several young players assumed key roles, including Joe Medwick, Ripper Collins, and a pair of pitching brothers from nearby Hannibal, Missouri, named Jerome and Paul Dean. He also dealt for a pugnacious little shortstop named Leo Durocher. When Durocher first got a load of his new teammates, he was taken aback by how loose they were and how crazy they acted.

The wild and wacky 1934 St. Louis Cardinals, winners of the 1934 World Series

But he also admired how mentally tough they were and how hard they played, calling them "gas house" ball players. Rickey, as ingenious a promoter as he was a judge of talent, liked this image and began feeding stories to the press that painted his Cardinals as a bunch of screwballs, drunks, and ne'er-do-wells who somehow came together as a team.

As the season unfolded, Jerome "Dizzy" Dean emerged as the best hurler in the league. Starting and relieving in 50 games, he won 30 and recorded seven shutouts. The good-natured righty also set unofficial records for bizarre quotes, tall tales, and crazy predictions. He and Paul, he boasted that spring, would win 45 games. Actually, they won 49, as Paul racked up 19, including a no-hitter. The offense clicked, too, with first baseman Collins leading the league in home runs and Medwick knocking in more than 100 runs and banging out a league-high 18 triples. During the season's final three days, the Dean brothers pitched 27 innings of one-run ball, and the Cardinals erased a one-game deficit to take the pennant.

This would be the one and only flag for the Gas House Gang. The Deans both suffered arm injuries, Frisch became a part-time player, and Collins had only one more good season. The guy who kept on going was Medwick, who in 1937 led the NL in runs, hits, doubles home runs, RBIs, batting, and slugging. Medwick was just one of a number of highly productive line-drive hitting outfielders in the National League during the 1930s. Chief among them was Paul Waner of the Pirates, who took full advantage of horseshoe-shaped Forbes Field. If outfielders positioned themselves in the park's immense power alleys, he would chip the ball down either foul line. If they tried to prevent this tactic, he would blast balls into the gaps.

Challenging Paul Waner for supremacy as the league's best rightfielder was Mel Ott of the New York Giants. The NL's top power hitter during the 1930s, Ott learned how to turn on the ball and send it down the line into the rightfield stands at the Polo Grounds less than 250 feet away. He led the league in homers five times during the 1930s and was so dangerous with men on that he was often walked intentionally even when there was not an open base. A regular at the age of 19, he was New York's starting rightfielder for 18 seasons and retired with 511 home runs.

Fans of the home run had a lot more to choose from in the AL, even after Babe Ruth left the Yankees following the 1934 season. Gehrig and Foxx won seven home run crowns between them during the decade, but right behind them was Hank Greenberg of the Tigers, who in any other era would have been a no-brainer as the best first baseman in baseball.

A tall, strong, left-handed hitter, he led Detroit to pennants in 1934 and 1935, hitting 63 doubles one year and knocking in 170 runs the next. In 1937, he collected 183 RBIs, and in 1938 he hit 58 home runs. Greenberg was also baseball's first Jewish superstar, and as such he was a great inspiration to the Jewish community during a difficult time. Greenberg liked to say that every time he hit a home run he was thumbing his nose at German dictator Adolf Hitler. Unfortunately, being Jewish may have worked against Greenberg. In 1937, he had 100 RBIs at the All-Star break yet was not selected for the team; for the season Greenberg hit 58 home runs and had a good chance to break Ruth's record of 60, but he was not given a decent pitch to hit during the season's final few games. The Tigers had another potent weapon in Charlie Gehringer, who offered sure-handed defense and highly productive offense. He won Detroit's second base job in 1926 and held it through 1941, leading the AL in runs, hits, and doubles twice each, as well as winning the 1937 batting title.

Rebuilding the Yankees

As for the Yankees, they won the pennant and World Series in 1932—getting one last great year out of Ruth—then set about the task of rebuilding the team around Gehrig. By 1936, the job was complete. Gehrig and second baseman Lazzeri were joined by a pair of capable players in shortstop Frank Crosetti and third baseman Red Rolfe. Bill Dickey had assumed the catching duties in 1929, establishing himself as the heir apparent to Mickey Cochrane as the league's best receiver. New York entrusted its pitching duties to Red Ruffing and Lefty Gomez.

What put the Yankees over the hump after three years of second-place finishes was the arrival of a young centerfielder from the West Coast. Joe DiMaggio had made news as a teenager with a 61-game hitting streak for the San Francisco Seals of the Pacific Coast League, but a knee injury scared away many teams. The Yankees took a chance on the kid and were handsomely rewarded when he produced a terrific rookie season in 1936. From his first year in the major leagues, anyone who knew anything about baseball could see "Joltin' Joe" was something special. DiMaggio's instincts—at bat, in the field, on the bases—were per-

Charlie Gehringer was an expert bunter as well as a great line-drive hitter. The second baseman was a mainstay in the Tigers lineup for 15 years.

fect. And he did everything with tremendous grace and almost no wasted motion. He got to fly balls no one else could yet never seemed to be running hard. He was aggressive on the bases, yet never seemed to get thrown out. And when DiMaggio swung, the lower half of his body barely moved, while the upper half twisted in a quick, fluid movement that produced rocket shots.

DiMaggio led the Yankees to four consecutive pennants and four world championships between 1936 and 1939 and was an All-Star every single year of his career. Although his statistics paled in comparison to his actual skills, DiMaggio's genius for baseball escaped no one. He played in the

Joe DiMaggio and his son appear on the cover of the very first *Sport* magazine. The Yankee centerfielder's 56-game hitting streak captivated the nation five years earlier.

worst possible stadium for his offensive tools and performed in an era when teams simply did not take advantage of what he had to offer. Still, at various times during New York's four-pennant streak, DiMaggio led the AL in runs, triples, home runs, RBIs, batting average, and slugging average.

Changing of the Guard

During the 1936 season, DiMaggio shared the headlines with another highly touted rookie. His name was Bob Feller, and he threw the ball as hard as anyone who had ever played the game. The Cleveland Indi-

ans discovered him throwing 100 miles an hour against a homemade backstop at his family's farm in Van Meter, Iowa, and signed him for a dollar and an autographed baseball. Feller was only 17, but he got his first major-league start that July and proceeded to strike out 15 St. Louis Browns. He also struck out 17 Athletics in a game that season. Feller was likely to fan any batter he faced, but just as likely to walk him. Even in 1938, when he went 17–11 and led the league with 240 strikeouts, Feller sometimes walked six or more men a game. In 1939, he finally got a grip on his control and posted a league-high 24 victories.

As the American League's new pitching sensation was ascending, the sun was setting on the career of the National League's top pitcher of the 1930s. Left-hander Carl Hubbell of the New York Giants threw a screwball, and he threw it better than anyone before or since. He used the pitch—which broke sharply down and away from righties and bored in on lefties—so often that by the end of the decade his arm was permanently twisted so that his palm faced outward when he let his left arm hang down at his side. Hubbell's ability to throw the screwball for strikes meant that batters were forced to swing at it; they could not wait for a 3-1 count and expect a fastball. The result was that "King Carl" held opponents to the lowest batting average in the league seven times in nine seasons. He struck out five future Hall of Famers in a row during the 1934 All-Star Game and pitched the Giants to the pennant in 1933. He got New York to the World Series again in 1936 and 1937 while also setting a two-season record by winning 24 consecutive games. A 1938 elbow operation limited him to 150 to 200 innings a year, but he continued to baffle hitters and post double-digit victory totals for five more seasons.

The Luckiest Man on the Face of the Earth

The 1930s closed on a couple of positive notes. A balance had been struck between hitting and pitching that seemed to work, and despite the near shutdown of the U.S. economy, baseball appeared to be surviving. Attendance had dropped to six million in 1933, but it had rebounded steadily each year, hovering around nine million from 1937 to 1939.

The 1939 season, however, was one of sadness. Lou Gehrig, who had played in 2,130 consecutive games despite high fevers, broken bones, and near exhaustion, pulled himself out of the Yankee lineup eight games into the schedule. He had been stricken by amyotrophic lateral sclerosis, an incurable disease that robbed him of his muscle coordination. Two years later it would take his life. The 36-year-old Yankee captain traveled with the team all year and suited up for every game, but he never played again. On July 4, he gave a touching farewell speech to a capacity crowd at Yankee Stadium. When he proclaimed himself "the luckiest man on the face of the earth" there was not a dry eye in the house. Gehrig was thanking baseball for giving him good friends, great memories, and a wonderful life. In a way, he captured the hold baseball had developed on the American psyche. It was the national game, and it had, in its own small way, helped pull a lot of people through a national crisis. The country was emerging from the Great Depression more

"SID" HUDSON

Pitcher Sid Hudson was one of the many emerging stars who lost their prime years to World War II.

or less intact, and the same could be said for baseball.

The 1940s

The United States went to war with Germany, Italy, and Japan at the end of 1941, meaning major-league baseball had just two full seasons before the majority of its players left for the service. By 1946, those who had any baseball left in them returned to the field, meaning there were four more or less complete seasons at the end of the decade. In the interim, between 1942 and 1945, the majors made do with what was available, and talent got pretty thin. But it was baseball, and just as it had buoyed the spirits of the nation during the Great Depression, the game would provide a welcome distraction both for the young soldiers fighting overseas and for the people working for the war effort at home.

The 1941 season was a wild one from beginning to end, and it gave fans some marvelous memories to carry them through the war years. In the National League, the Dodgers and the Cardinals were at each other's throats all summer long, with Brooklyn squeezing out the pennant by the slimmest of margins. After two decades of futility, the team had risen to prominence thanks to general manager Larry MacPhail, a protégé of Branch Rickey and a shrewd and daring executive in his own right. Feeling the Dodgers lacked leadership, he traded for first baseman Dolph Camilli, a strong, silent slugger who impressed many in the league with his steady defense and keen understanding of the game. To manage the team, MacPhail selected high-strung Leo Durocher, who was nearing the end of his effectiveness as a player when he joined the Dodgers in 1939. He, too, had a good baseball mind and would serve as an interesting counter-balance to the quiet Camilli. In 1940, MacPhail added a pair of promising 21-year-old shortstops, Pee Wee Reese and Pete Reiser. Both became regulars in 1941, with Reese staying at shortstop and Reiser moving to centerfield. Reiser, batting third, captured the batting crown and made one spectacular game-saving play after another at his new position. He had as much raw talent as anyone in the league, and his go-for-broke approach made him the most-watched player on the field. With veteran Joe Medwick batting behind cleanup hitter Camilli, the Dodger offense was hard to contain. The team's pitching was nothing to sneer at, either. The Brooklyn staff boasted

the NL's top two winners in scatter-armed Kirby Higbe and notorious headhunter Whitlow Wyatt, while hard-living, hard-throwing Hugh Casey came out of the bullpen.

In the AL, the New York Yankees had added some impressive new players to the team that won four straight pennants in the late 1930s. At second base, Joe Gordon provided even more punch than Lazzeri had, and his keystone partner, Phil Rizzuto, hit .307 in his first full season to make the fans forget all about Crosetti. The team had also improved in left, where Charlie "King Kong" Keller lived up to his nickname by blasting 33 home runs, and in right, where Tommy Henrich chipped in 31 round-trippers and specialized in dramatic, game-winning hits. But the big story on the Yanks that year—in fact, the biggest story in all of sports—was Joe DiMaggio, who captured the nation's attention with a record 56-game hitting streak. From mid-May to mid-July, "Joltin' Joe" managed at least one hit in every game, and every evening the question on the lips of everyone in America was "Did Joe get a hit today?" When the Cleveland Indians finally halted DiMaggio's streak, he began another one that lasted 16 more games.

In the World Series, the Dodgers played the Yankees tough and appeared to have knotted matters at two games apiece when Casey fanned Henrich in the ninth inning of the fourth game. But the ball eluded catcher Mickey Owen and Henrich reached first, igniting a game-winning rally. Owen may have been crossed up by Casey (who was known to ignore signs and even throw an occasional spitter), but the play is still considered the costliest blunder in post-season history. Up three games to one, New York went for the jugular and ended the series in five games.

The 1941 season belonged to the arrival of the best young hitter anyone had ever seen, Ted Williams of the Boston Red Sox. He captured the Triple Crown that year, won the All-Star Game with two out in the bottom of the ninth, and also became the last player to bat .400. Hovering just .00045 below the hallowed mark as he entered the final day of the season, he went six-for-eight to end up at .406. Williams was obsessed with the science of hitting, refusing to swing at any pitch that was not a strike. A cocky young outfielder who came from a dysfunctional family background, he had a difficult time dealing with others, particularly the fans and the press. Williams once commented that he would prefer to play in an empty ballpark, and he was known to spit on reporters he did not like. Thus as great as he was—and some say he was the best hitter ever—"The Splendid Splinter" was not one of baseball's most beloved individuals.

Tigers slugger Hank Greenberg, pictured here at an army camp in Michigan, was the first of the many top players who entered the armed forces during World War II.

The Lean Years

When the United States was drawn into World War II, scores of players from the majors and minors enlisted immediately. During the course of the 1942 season, when the war was going badly for the United States, hundreds more joined. And by 1943, everyone who was able to soldier was doing so, leaving the major leagues with just a handful of stars to carry it through some very lean years. The only ball players left were the very young, the very old, and those who received military deferments for physical conditions such as bulging disks and irregular heartbeats. One-dimensional players who would have barely qualified as major league hangers-on suddenly became starters. Veterans whose best days were far behind them were pressed back into service until their bodies literally gave out. Needless to say, the quality of play was not very good. Even the quality of the ball was down, probably because all the good yarn was being used for army blankets and other pressing war needs. Whatever the difference, from 1942 to 1945, it took a Herculean effort to hit a home run. That was lucky for the pitchers, because there were not too many capable of keeping the ball in the park under normal conditions. Ironically, speed became a valuable commodity once again, especially on the base paths, where runs actually had to be "manufactured" for the first time in more than 20 years. And the concept of relief pitching took an important step forward, as the lack of young, healthy starters forced managers to work their bullpens with a little more savvy.

Few of the standout performers during the war years proved themselves to be legitimate stars once the real players started coming back in 1946. In the American League, such unfamiliar names as George Case, Vern Stephens, Jeff Heath, Nick Etten, and Snuffy Stirnweiss appeared among the leaders in the offensive categories, while unheralded hurlers Dizzy Trout, Jack Kramer, Spud Chandler, and Dutch Leonard counted themselves among the league's most reliable hurlers. Only two big-time players distinguished themselves in the AL during the war, Lou Boudreau and Hal Newhouser. In 1942, Boudreau became player-manager of the Indians at the age of 24. He was a sure-handed shortstop with a potent bat who proved just as good after the war as during it. Newhouser was the dominant player in baseball during the war years, winning 29 and 25 games in 1944 and 1945, respectively. He was elected the AL MVP in both seasons, and he continued to pitch well after World War II, winning 26 in 1946 and 21 in 1948. Although Newhouser's career stats were somewhat flawed because of the low caliber of wartime competition, there was no denying that he would have been a superb pitcher in any era.

Over in the National League, the picture was very much the same. For four years, fans were treated to the exploits of Dixie Walker, Tommy Holmes, Phil Cavaretta, Augie Galan, Bob Elliott, and Bill Nicholson—all perfectly good offensive players, but nothing special. The pitching stars included Harry Brecheen, Mort Cooper, Rip Sewell, and Claude Passeau. They were a talented bunch, but not very exciting. The only major star to come into his own in the NL was Stan Musial of the St. Louis Cardinals. During the late-1930s, he was just another minor-league pitcher plagued by control problems. Hoping to find another way to stay in baseball, Musial spent his off-days learning how to hit and play the outfield with the Daytona Beach club of the

NOT FOR MEN ONLY

In 1943, with the top names in the big leagues off to war, Cubs owner Phil Wrigley bankrolled a professional softball league for women. The rules were altered to give batters a big advantage, and stealing was permitted. The idea was to attract fans who wanted to see good baseball and pretty faces—a combination definitely not offered at the major-league level. By 1944, the All-American Girls Baseball League had traded its softball for a hardball, and thus began an experiment that lasted until 1954.

WAR WITH MEXICO

In 1946, millionaire Jorge Pasquel attempted to elevate the Mexican League to major-league status by signing players who were returning after the war. He also pursued several black players, who were still barred from the majors. Because the Mexican League was not part of the National Agreement, it was not compelled to recognize baseball's reserve clause, and that meant open season on any player who would listen to offers. Several did make the move to Mexico, including eight members of the New York Giants, who ended up finishing the 1946 season dead last. Commissioner Happy Chandler promised to bar any league-jumpers for five years, and the threat stemmed the tide of talent headed south of the border. Still, nearly two dozen potential major-league regulars were lost to Pasquel, including highly regarded pitchers Max Lanier and Sal Maglie.

Florida State League in 1940. Late in the 1940 season, he dove for a ball in the outfield and crushed his left shoulder. The injury ended his pitching career and would prove serious enough to keep him out of the service for most of the war. In 1941, Musial tore up minor-league pitching and made it all the way to the majors, hitting .426 for St. Louis after a mid-September call-up. By his second season he had established himself as the best hitter in the league. With "Stan the Man" leading the way the Cardinals won the pennant every year from 1942 to 1944. A line-drive hitter who developed home-run power after the war, Musial twisted his body while awaiting a pitch then uncoiled in a smooth, explosive stroke as the ball crossed the plate.

World War II ended in time for most former big leaguers to obtain their discharges and get in some spring training before the 1946 season started. The hitters were ahead of the pitchers, who struggled to regain their control. Thus the common wisdom among batters was to wait for a perfect pitch before swinging. This resulted in an unprecedented number of walks—a trend which continued for many years, especially in the American League, where there were nearly nine walks a game in 1948 and nearly ten a game in 1949.

With the players and fans back home for the 1946 season, attendance leaped from 10.8 million to 18.5 million. This figure continued to rise until it leveled off at 20 million in 1948 and 1949; it was helped by some of the greatest pennant races in history. In 1946, the Cardinals and Dodgers finished the season tied with 96 wins, making necessary a three-game playoff, which was won by the Cards. In 1948, the Indians and Red Sox finished dead even at 96 wins, with the Indians winning the first playoff in American League history. And in 1949, both leagues saw the pennant decided on the final day, with the Yankees stealing the flag from the Red Sox and the Dodgers finishing strong to edge the Cardinals.

New York managers had the toughest jobs in baseball. Here, Joe McCarthy, Mel Ott, and Leo Durocher (left to right) appear on this April 1946 cover of *Baseball Magazine*.

The four big bats of the Boston line-up—Ted Williams, Bobby Doerr, Dom DiMaggio, and Vern Stephens—grace the cover of the January 1949 *Baseball Magazine*.

The Color Barrier Falls

In the spring of 1945, Branch Rickey—by this time the general manager of the Brooklyn Dodgers—set in motion a plan to break baseball's color barrier. Rickey was driven by two desires. First and foremost, he believed the best players in the Negro Leagues were every bit as good as those in the majors, and that meant he could build a Dodger dynasty if he got his foot in the door and signed the best black talent before his competitors. Second, he had long been haunted by the memory of an experience from his college days at Ohio Wesleyan University,

when he managed the baseball team. Rickey's top star back then was Tommy Thomas, a black first baseman. In a game against Kentucky, the Wildcat players had refused to play OWU, instructing Rickey to "Get that nigger off the field." Rickey held his ground and the game was eventually played. Thomas, however, was humiliated, and later he broke down and cried. Rickey remembered his star weeping and rubbing his hands over and over, wishing he could make his skin white.

Rickey suspected the world was ready for a black baseball player, but he knew he would have to choose a special person. He would have to be a very good player, but

THE COLOR BARRIER

There was no specific rule barring black players, but none had been allowed to play in organized baseball since 1887, when a black pitcher named George Stovey seemed on the verge of greatness with Newark of the International League. Stovey was scheduled to pitch an exhibition game against Chicago, but Cap Anson refused to play, feigning illness. A short while later, when John Ward suggested the New York Giants sign Stovey, Anson—the most powerful player in the league—protested so strongly that the matter was dropped. Eventually, the players in the International League followed suit and drove Stovey from the game. In the six decades that followed, the only other attempt to sign a black player was made by Baltimore's John McGraw. He tried to pass off Charlie Grant as an American Indian in spring training of 1901, but Charles Comiskey blew the whistle on him.

just as important, he would have to be able to endure all the pressures that went with the opportunity. This search took some time, and Rickey's scouts were easily spotted in the stands during Negro National League games. To explain their presence, Rickey announced that he was forming a new "clean" league for black players, which would take the game out of the hands of the "numbers kings" and replace them with legitimate backers. It was an elaborate ruse, but it worked. After considering several top players, Rickey decided that Jackie Robinson was the perfect candidate. Robinson was not the best player in the Negro Leagues, nor was he particularly fond of baseball. In fact, he was playing shortstop for the Kansas City Monarchs strictly for the money, about $100 a week.

In August, Rickey summoned Robinson to his office, and the Dodger GM revealed his plan. He spent several hours trying to get Robinson to understand the kind of pressures he would be facing. Rickey told him he could not fight back, no matter how many runners spiked him, no matter how many pitchers threw at him, and no matter how much verbal abuse was directed his way. Robinson considered all that was on the table and decided that if Rickey was willing to take a chance on him, he would promise to hold back no matter how tough the going got. Two months later, the Dodgers announced that Robinson had been signed by Brooklyn's top farm team, the Montreal Royals of the International League. All winter long, the Robinson signing was all anyone in baseball could talk about. Some baseball people were for it, believing it was time to right an ancient wrong. But most players and team officials—particularly those raised in the south—thought it was a ridiculous idea. Black men just could not play major-league baseball, they insisted, and that was all there was to it.

Robinson began to change people's

After winning the MVP award in 1949, Jackie Robinson signs a new contract as Dodgers president Branch Rickey looks on.

minds from his very first game with the Royals in the spring of 1946, when he collected four hits, including a three-run homer. In that game, he also stole two bases and scored twice by dancing off third base and making the pitcher balk. It was, in every way, a preview of what Robinson would be bringing to the Dodgers a year later. He led the Royals to the International League title in 1946 and was the star of the Little World Series, the championship of minor-league baseball. After the clinching game, jubilant Montreal fans spotted Robinson on the street and began chasing after him to show their appreciation. Not sure what to do—there being something of a hard, fast rule where white mobs were concerned—Robinson ran for his life.

Robinson was promoted to the Dodgers for the 1947 season. This development touched off a brief rebellion on the team, as a group of southern players drew up a petition stating they preferred to be traded than to play with a black man. Shortstop Pee Wee Reese, a Kentucky native, refused to go along, saying that if Robinson could take his job, he was entitled to it. At Rickey's behest, manager Leo Durocher got together with the offended players prior to the season and put it to them in terms they could understand: Robinson was a heck of a ballplayer, and if they just shut their mouths and played baseball the new fellow was going to make them all rich. Robinson did not take Reese's job—he played first base that year—but he quickly established himself as the top player on the team. He batted .297, led the league in stolen bases, and was voted Rookie of the

In this Ron Lewis oil painting, Hall-of-Famer Monte Irvin is pictured in his Newark Eagles (Negro National League) uniform. Irvin joined the NL Giants in 1949.

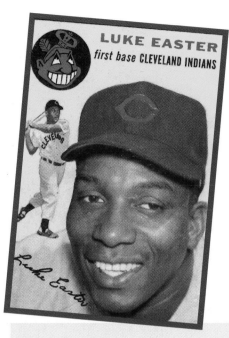

Luke Easter was one of the early African-American players in the major leagues. He started playing for the Indians in 1949 at age 34.

Year. And true to Durocher's word, the Dodgers all cashed fat World Series checks that fall, as they won the NL pennant.

Within a few seasons, everyone who had expressed doubts about the qualifications of black ballplayers had to admit they were wrong. Not only were Robinson and the African-Americans who followed him as good as major leaguers, on the balance they were better. Baseball had become a slow, stagnant game after the war, with a lot of walks and an over-reliance on the home run. Robinson brought with him from the Negro National League an intense and aggressive approach that invigorated the game and made him its most dynamic player. In 1949, he won the batting title and MVP award, and for the next few years no one in baseball was a better all-around player.

Following Robinson to the majors were more big names from the Negro National League. In July of 1947, Larry Doby, a star with the Newark Eagles, broke in with the Cleveland Indians, and Hank Thompson, a teammate of Robinson's on the Monarchs, stepped onto the field for the St. Louis Browns. In 1948, catcher Roy Campanella, a huge star with the Baltimore Elite Giants, joined Robinson on the Dodgers, and Satchel Paige—another former Monarch and the most celebrated pitcher in Negro League history—helped the Indians win the American League pennant. In 1949, the parade continued, with the Dodgers adding pitcher Don Newcombe, the Giants signing slugger Monte Irvin, and the Indians inking Luke Easter. A great many young black players were also performing on the minor-league level, and they would soon be arriving in the majors in significant numbers.

The Yankees-Dodgers Rivalry

With the exception of Jackie Robinson and a handful of other daring players, baseball during the 1950s went through the most conservative era in its history. Interestingly, the United States was going through a similar period. There was a tremendous fear of anything new or even remotely radical; the prospect of change made people downright paranoid. America was in the throes of its Cold War with the Soviet Union, and everyone was afraid that someone—them or us—might drop the "big one," a nuclear bomb, at any moment. The threat of the big one also gripped baseball, too. Every team had to have its own B-52 clean-up hitter capable of dropping a bomb into the bleachers, ideally with a couple of runners on base. Pitching strategy was just as straightforward and uninspired: basically, the idea was to keep the other team from hitting home runs. With everyone swinging for the fences, doubles, triples, and batting averages dropped steadily. Unless you were rooting for the Yankees or the Dodgers, the 1950s were one big yawn.

That was because New York and Brooklyn were the only two teams that did not play straight-up, classic 1950s baseball. The Dodgers fulfilled Branch Rickey's dream of a multiracial dynasty, winning the NL pennant four times in seven years and challenging right down to the last day of the season on two other occasions. Jackie Robinson eventually settled in at second base, making way for first baseman Gil Hodges, a sure-handed fielder who hit between 22 and 42 home runs a season during the 1950s and drove home 100-plus runs each year from 1949 to 1955. Carl Furillo was no slouch at the plate, either. He consistently batted. 290 to .300 and surprised everyone in 1953 when his average soared to .344 and he won the batting crown. A master at playing the tricky bounces off Ebbets Field's rightfield fence, Furillo cut down countless runners with his strong arm over the years, giving the Dodgers a very unique and definite home-field advantage.

Joining Robinson, Hodges, and Furillo to give Brooklyn great power from the right side was Roy Campanella. He had some monster years with the bat, but it was behind the plate where he did his best work, handling Brooklyn's sometimes-shaky pitching staff and fielding his position with quickness and grace. Campanella was recognized for his fine play with three Most Valuable Player awards. Those who support him as history's top catcher point to the MVPs, but they also bring up the fact that he had been catching for more than 10 years in the Negro National and Mexican Leagues before joining the Dodgers in 1948. In other words, Campanella was the world's best catchers for more than a dozen years. In January 1958, his car flipped over and crushed his spine, ending his career and leaving him wheelchair-bound for the rest of his life. The Dodgers kept opposing righties honest with Duke Snider, the NL's top left-handed power threat during the 1950s. Unlike other sluggers, however, Snider concentrated on hitting the ball where it was pitched and hitting it hard. The result was a lot of extra-base hits, runs, and RBIs. Snider was also recognized for his glovework in centerfield, and he made the

The 1955 Brooklyn Dodgers won the World Series against their crosstown rivals, the Yankees.

All-Star team every year from 1950 to 1956. He also hit 40 or more home runs every year from 1953 to 1957.

Brooklyn could beat you with the home run or the stolen base, and they could single you to death. And somehow, they always seemed to have a pitcher who was on a roll. In the early 1950s it was either old-timer Preacher Roe or Don Newcombe, an imposing power pitcher whose fastball exploded as it reached the plate. Newcombe was the first really good black pitcher in major-league history, and the Dodgers had to scramble for wins when he spent 1952 and 1953 in the army. Newk returned and led the Dodgers to their first world championship in 1955, then posted a 27–7 mark in 1956. In the mid-1950s, Carl Erskine was the class of the Brooklyn staff, despite pitching in intense pain every time out. He had injured his arm as a rookie in 1948 but learned to survive by changing speeds on his fastball and curve. The staff's lifesaver was Clem Labine, who used a sharp sinker

to baffle enemy hitters. From 1954 to 1959, he appeared in at least 45 games a season and led the National League in saves in 1956 and 1957. Labine was also selected for the NL All-Star team twice—a rare honor in the days before pitchers got much credit for their work out of the bullpen.

The Yankees also won with speed, power, defense, and timely pitching. But they had something the Dodgers did not— Casey Stengel, a manager with some definite ideas on utilizing his personnel. Stengel had been a good player in the 1920s, though a bit of a strange character. In the 1930s he found his way into managing, serving as skipper of the Dodgers and Braves during their most dismal years. During the late 1940s, however, Casey atoned for his past sins and developed a reputation as a progressive skipper in the minor leagues. Still, when the Yankees hired him in 1949 it raised a lot of eyebrows.

Stengel implemented a sophisticated platoon system and guided the team to a

MIGHTY CASEY

Today, platooning is not considered unusual, but back in the 1950s Stengel was its main practitioner. This gave him a terrific advantage. Not only could he keep an assortment of fresh bodies in the lineup, but he could pluck a pair of .240 hitters off other teams, alternate them at the same spot, and end up with a .300 average, 25 homers, and 100 RBIs from that position. The Yankee platoon squad during the 1950s included Billy Johnson, Hank Bauer, Gene Woodling, Bobby Brown, Bob Cerv, Irv Noren, Andy Carey, Moose Skowron, Joe Collins, Billy Martin, Elston Howard, Jerry Coleman, and Gil McDougald. All were good players, but none of them was great. They all griped about playing time, but at season's end, when the World Series checks came, they were glad they stuck with Casey. From 1949 to 1960, Stengel's Yankees won a mind-boggling 10 pennants in 12 years.

pennant that, on paper, they should not have won. If he did not have someone who could play every day, he simply used two or three players at that position. And when he rested one of his everyday players, he made sure it was against a pitcher he had trouble hitting—and that he replaced his regular with someone who had been successful against that same hurler.

Stengel's regulars were great players, of course. Doing most of the catching was Yogi Berra, the man opponents hated to see at bat in the late innings of a tight game. He could not be pitched to, and he could not be pitched around, because he swung at (and usually hit) anything within a foot of the strike zone. From 1949 to 1955, he led the team in RBIs each season, despite sharing the lineup with a half-dozen Hall of Famers. Like Campanella, he won three MVPs during the decade. At shortstop, the Yankees featured a valuable sparkplug in Phil Riz-

zuto. A smart fielder and excellent situational hitter, he was dubbed the most important player on the Yankees by no less an authority than Ted Williams. In 1950, "The Scooter" batted .324 and led the league in fielding to win the AL Most Valuable Player award.

Stengel also exhibited a deft touch in the handling of his pitching staff, which changed significantly from year to year. The constant was Whitey Ford, a smart, tough left-hander who managed to win big despite a lack of overpowering stuff. He mixed his pitches brilliantly, never giving in to a hitter and rarely catching more than an inch or two of the plate. When runners did reach base against Ford, he kept them close to the bag with the league's best pickoff move, and he fielded bunts well enough to nail runners before they got to second base. Year in and year out, he won more than half of his starts with an ERA in the 2.00s, and only once during the 1950s did he lose more than eight games. What ultimately distinguished Ford as the AL's best pitcher, though, was that he was at his very best in big games, especially in World Series play.

Ford was surrounded by other talented hurlers, including Allie Reynolds, Vic Raschi, and Eddie Lopat. Reynolds turned in eight superb seasons after being acquired from the Indians in a 1947 trade that sent Joe Gordon to Cleveland. He threw hard but was resilient enough to pitch relief on little rest. Stengel used Reynolds six times as a reliever in World Series play, and each time "The Big Chief" recorded either a win or a save, which is pretty impressive. The author of two no-hitters during the 1951 season, he won the Hickock Belt as America's top pro athlete that year and would have won the Cy Young Award had it existed back then. Raschi was another hard thrower, and he won 111 games for the Yankees during his six seasons as a starter. Lopat gave the Yanks a different look, with his assortment of off-speed junk and breaking balls. Stengel usually inserted him between Reynolds and Raschi. Lopat ate the free-swingers of the 1950s alive, keeping them off balance and never throwing anything that was remotely as good as it looked. He averaged 16 wins a year from 1949 to 1953 and won the ERA title in 1953.

In the late 1950s, Stengel went with whoever had the hot hand, getting great seasons out of several pitchers who were only slightly better than average. Ranging from unknown youngsters to grizzled vets, they included Bob Turley, Tom Sturdivant, Bobby Shantz, Johnny Kucks, Tommy Byrne, Bob Grim, and Don Larsen, who fashioned a perfect game in the 1956 World Series. Most turned in one or two good

Yogi Berra, Whitey Ford, and Mickey Mantle of the Yankees played together on 10 pennant winners.

years and then faded away, but their contributions enabled the team to nail down four pennants in a row from 1955 to 1958.

The big gun on the New York Yankee teams of the 1950s was centerfielder Mickey Mantle. After a decent rookie year in 1951, the 21-year-old moved over from rightfield to replace the retiring Joe DiMaggio. Mantle stayed there for 15 seasons, playing through the intense pain of a degenerative bone disease called osteomyelitis. In the few seasons he stayed free of major injuries, he was baseball's best offensive player, hitting for a high average and clubbing 500-foot home runs from both sides of the plate. In his early years, he was the fastest runner in baseball; later, he developed into a fearsome clutch hitter. In 1956 Mantle put together a season for the ages— 52 homers, 130 RBIs and a .353 average— to win the Triple Crown and the American League MVP. It was in the locker room,

Many fans consider Willie Mays to be baseball's best all-around player ever.

however, where Mantle may have had his biggest impact on the Yanks. When his teammates watched the agony he endured each day in order to play, they too were determined to leave everything they had on the field.

Willie, Ernie, and Hank

Challenging Mantle and Snider for supremacy among major-league centerfielders in the 1950s was Willie Mays of the Giants, the best all-around player in the National League from 1954 on. He brought to the game the same kind of speed, daring, and instincts that Jackie Robinson did but added to this package awesome power. Mays not only did everything well, he did everything with the kind of passion and excitement that was so lacking from baseball during the

1950s. He also reawakened the idea that a running attack could be just as effective as the power game. His first two seasons with the Giants were 1951 and 1954 (he was in the military for all but 34 games in 1952 and 1953), and it was no coincidence that the team won the pennant both years.

In 1951, the Giants started 1–11 and called Mays up from the minors in May. Despite his considerable contributions, New York still trailed Brooklyn by 13 games in mid-August. Then the whole team kicked it into overdrive, tying the Dodgers with seven straight victories to end the season. The Giants and Dodgers split the first two games of the ensuing three-game playoff, and the Dodgers held a 5-3 lead with one out in the bottom of the ninth of the deciding third game. Ralph Branca was called upon to relieve Don Newcombe, and two pitches later he gave up a pennant-winning three-run homer to Bobby Thomson that became known as "The Shot Heard 'Round the World." Thomson, who began the year as the Giants centerfielder, was moved to third by Leo Durocher when young Mays came to New York.

Mays had his breakout year in 1954, batting .345 with 41 home runs, and the Giants swept to their second pennant in four seasons. In the World Series, they faced the heavily favored Cleveland Indians. The underdog Giants looked to be on the ropes in the opener when Cleveland slugger Vic Wertz launched a 460-foot drive to centerfield with two men on and the score tied 2-2. But the amazing Mays, running with the crack of the bat, raced under the ball and made an incredible catch with his back to home plate. He wheeled and fired to the infield to complete a double play, and the Giants won the game in extra innings. Then, against all odds, the Giants went on to sweep the Indians in four games.

Mays was the finest of many black players who found their way to the National League during the 1950s. The same year Mays made his great World Series catch, Ernie Banks took over at shortstop for the Chicago Cubs, and Hank Aaron got an unexpected shot in the Milwaukee Braves outfield. Banks was something baseball had never seen before: a Gold Glove–caliber shortstop who could bat .300, hit 40 home runs, and drive in 100 runs a season. Sadly for Banks, he spent his prime years surrounded by mediocre players, and the team never had a winning season during the 1950s. Still, in 1958 and 1959, Banks had such incredible seasons (47 and 45 homers, 129 and 143 RBIs) that he was voted the MVP despite the fact that the Cubs finished fifth each time. Aaron, an infielder both in the Negro National League and the minors, got a shot at rightfield in 1954 when Bobby Thomson (acquired from the Giants in a winter deal) broke his leg during spring training. Aaron won the job and, within two years, he was one of the top hitters in baseball. "Hammerin' Hank" used his quick, strong wrists to whip his bat through the hitting zone and produce some of the hardest line drives anyone had ever seen. He was aggressive when he had to be but generally played with a laid-back, understated style. This approach enabled him to avoid injury and remain one of baseball's most productive hitters for two decades. In 1957, Aaron led the NL in runs, homers, and RBIs to win the MVP, and he got the Braves into the World Series with a pennant-clinching home run against the St. Louis Cardinals. He continued his hot hitting against the Yankees in the 1957 World Series, leading a

"Mr. Cub" Ernie Banks chats with a group of young fans in Chicago.

remarkable comeback that saw the Braves erase a 3–1 deficit and win it all in seven games.

Pitching Stars of the 1950s

With all the slugging going on in baseball, it took an extraspecial pitcher to win with any consistency. In the National League, Robin Roberts of the Philadelphia Phillies ranked as the top right-hander of the decade. In 1950, he went 20–11 with five shutouts to help the "Whiz Kids" win the pennant, then won between 19 and 27 games over each of the next six seasons. Roberts did not fool around on the mound—he fired his hopping fastball across the plate and dared opponents to hit it. He gave up a lot of home runs, but few with men on base and even fewer when it mattered. The best lefty in the league during the 1950s was Warren Spahn. He was about as smart a pitcher as there was, and he blended his intelligence with an arm that could make a baseball do whatever he wanted. He had a darting fastball, a big curve, a tight little slider, and a devastating screwball, which became his best pitch when he started to lose the zip on his heater. If winning 20 games is the mark of a good pitcher, then Spahn was something beyond good, for he won 20 or more an incredible 13 times. He led the Braves to three pennants and topped the league in just about every pitching category at one time or another. When he retired, he had 363 victories—the most of any southpaw in major-league history.

The pitching story over in the American League was all about the Indians. The team boasted four terrific starters in Bob Feller, Bob Lemon, Early Wynn, and Mike Garcia. Though at the tail end of his career, Feller continued to throw smoke until he was 35 and led the league in wins for the sixth and last time in 1951. Lemon, a sinker ball specialist, came into his own during the 1948 season, and he and Feller took the Indians to the World Series. In 1949, this trio was joined by Wynn, who had developed a legendary mean streak while pitching for the Senators during some lean years in the 1940s. It was said that he would knock down his own grandmother if she were crowding the plate. Garcia joined the starting rotation at the end of 1949, and from 1951 to 1954, this quartet was good for around 75 wins a year. In 1954, they were joined by sinkerballer Art Houtteman, whose career had been sidetracked by a stretch in the army, a fractured skull, and the death of his baby in a car crash. This quintet won 93 games, with help from a pair of hot relievers, Don Mossi and Ray Narleski. The result was 111 wins—a mark that no team has ever topped, even when the schedule was expanded from 154 games to the present 162 games.

The offense for that team was supplied by Larry Doby and Al Rosen. As the American League's first black player, Doby had been subjected to much the same kind of prejudice as Jackie Robinson, but his playing style and personality were not nearly as antagonistic as Robinson's. That did not mean Doby was not a fierce competitor; he just got the job done a little less flamboyantly. The patient, clutch hitting he had displayed back with the Newark Eagles carried over into the majors. Between 1950 and 1956, Doby topped 100 RBIs each season and led the AL in home runs and RBIs during that marvelous 1954 campaign. Rosen, the regular at third base for the Indians from 1950 to 1956, was one of the most devastating hitters of his era. During those seven seasons, he averaged more than 27 homers and 100 RBIs. He, too, led the league in round-trippers twice and won the MVP award in 1953, when he missed the Triple Crown by a single hit. A nagging case of whiplash curbed Rosen's productivity in 1955 and 1956. When Cleveland fans began to boo him, he figured the heck with it and quit baseball at the age of 32.

The Splendid Splinter

Besides all those Yankee pennants, the one constant throughout the 1950s in the AL was the hitting of Ted Williams. Although he failed to dominate baseball the way he had in the 1940s, he was still a remarkable player. Unfortunately, Williams was usually surrounded by lackluster hitters, so pitchers rarely gave him much to swing at. In 1954 he was walked so many times that he failed to amass enough official at bats to qualify for the batting title, which he otherwise would have won. In 1955, he was walked 91 times in 98 games, despite being hampered by four different injuries. When teammate Jackie Jensen started putting up MVP-type numbers in the late 1950s, Williams finally began to get a little less respect and see a few more 3-1 fastballs. The old man made the pitchers pay. In 1957, Williams nearly hit .400 again at the age of 39, settling for a league-high .388. A fluke? Apparently not, for "The Splendid Splinter" copped the 1958 batting crown, too!

Hitting Stars of the 1950s

Among the more notable hitters in the NL during the 1950s were Stan Musial and Red Schoendienst of the Cardinals, Eddie Mathews and Joe Adcock of the Braves, and Del Ennis and Richie Ashburn of the Phillies. Musial, the league's dominant hitter in the late 1940s, continued to win batting titles throughout the 1950s. He took the crown in 1950, 1951 and 1952, and then again in 1957, when he was 36 years old. Musial had another great year in 1958, then hung on until 1963. He finished his career with 3,630 hits, and became the only grandfather in history to hit a home run. Schoendienst, a second baseman, established himself with the Cards after the war and developed into one of the league's top table-setters. In his twelfth season with St. Louis, the team dealt him to the Giants, who turned around and traded him to the Braves in 1957. Schoendienst proved to be the final ingredient for a

Ted Williams was a perfectionist when it came to his bats. The Splendid Splinter's legendary swing carried him to six AL batting championships.

Milwaukee club that had finished second two years in a row. He led the league in hits and fielding, helping the Braves dump the Cardinals down the stretch for their first of two straight pennants.

Schoendienst joined a team that was packed with power hitters. Aaron was the hardest to get out, but the two most feared sluggers for the Braves were Mathews and Adcock, who played third and first, respectively. Despite playing in a poor home run park, Mathews hit 40 or more four times during the decade, and drew a ton of walks. There was talk for a while about Mathews breaking Babe Ruth's all-time mark of 714 career home runs, but he tapered off in his 30s after leading the league for the last time with 46 in 1959. Hitting behind Mathews for 10 years was Adcock. He was typical of the sluggers of the 1950s—big, slow hulking fellows like Ted Kluszewski, Ralph Kiner, Hank Sauer, Vic Wertz, Roy Sievers and Gus Zernial—but with a couple of interesting exceptions. Adcock was remarkably resilient, bouncing back from serious injuries several times. And he also responded well when he was platooned. But the thing for which Adcock is most remembered is the game of games he enjoyed against the Dodgers in 1956, when he clubbed four homers and a double to set the all-time record with 18 total bases. Adcock ended up playing 17 seasons, and when he retired only six right handers had hit more home runs.

Richie Ashburn and Del Ennis helped the young Philadelphia Phillies win the 1950 National League pennant, and then spent the rest of the decade waiting for lightning to strike twice. It never did, but both men played brilliantly nonetheless. Ashburn was a fast, sure-handed center-fielder who matched great defense with a knack for getting on base. He had almost no power but made up for that by winning a pair of batting titles and finishing second on three other occasions. Ennis was the Philadelphia RBI man, establishing himself as one of the best clutch hitters in baseball. He was not much to look at in the outfield or on the bases, but he gave the team its one consistent power threat until he was traded to St. Louis late in his career.

The Indians and Yankees did not have the market on hitters cornered in the American League during the 1950s. The Tigers had a pair of young guns in Harvey Kuenn and Al Kaline. Kuenn did the impossible as a rookie in 1953, leading the league with 209 hits and playing a mean shortstop at the age of 22. But that was nothing compared to what his teammate did two seasons later. Kaline took the AL by surprise in 1955 when, at the age of 20, he won the batting title by 21 points. He had made the Tigers straight out of high school in 1953 based mainly on his defensive skills in rightfield. But a batting title? It still seems impossible. Although he never won another batting crown, Kaline developed into one of the most consistent all-around hitters in baseball, as well as the best defensive right-fielder in AL history. Kuenn would go on to lead the league in hits three more times, and would be the centerpiece of one of the biggest trades ever when he was dealt to the Indians after winning the 1959 batting title.

The man for whom Kuenn was traded was Rocky Colavito, and he happened to be the 1959 home-run champ. To this day, Indians fans believe that the transaction somehow touched off three decades of losing. The people of Cleveland loved Rocky, even when he hit one of his legendary slumps.

Fans roared in awe when he hit homers—he reached 300 faster than all but four men—and screamed with delight when he gunned down runners from his post in right field. A big swinger who actually became a true slugger when he learned to cut down on his stroke, Colavito made himself an excellent all-around player by the age of 22 and continued to perform at a high level for another decade. That same winter, the Indians also traded away Minnie Minoso, the most exciting black player in the league during the 1950s. At the beginning of the decade, he was among the leaders in triples and stolen bases each year. In 1954, he added a little extra pop and led the league in slugging. The ageless Minoso (he led the league in hits) spent most of his career with the White Sox and even made token appearances as a pinch-hitter at the ages of 53 and 57 to become the only man to play in five different decades. If the Indians could take back one trade, however, it would probably be the one they made in 1958, when they acquired a talented defensive first baseman named Vic Power. There was nothing wrong with Power—he was a two-time All-Star in four seasons with Cleveland—but the 23-year-old outfielder they sent to the Athletics would come back to haunt them as a member of the dreaded Yankees. His name was Roger Maris.

The Go-Go Sox

In a final twist of irony, the decade that lived by the home run ended up dying by the home run. In 1959, the Chicago White Sox, the only team in baseball not to hit 100 homers, took the AL pennant. The "Go-Go Sox" won the old-fashioned way, with pitching, defense, bunts, stolen bases, and

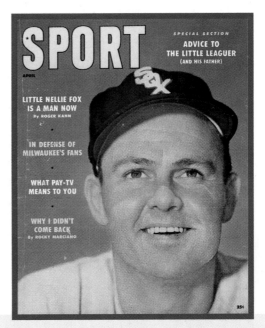

Nellie Fox appears on the cover of the April 1959 *Sport* magazine. Fox won the MVP that season and was inducted into the Hall of Fame in 1997.

hit-and-runs. Their leadoff man was Venezuelan shortstop Luis Aparicio, who almost single-handedly reintroduced the stolen base to baseball during the latter part of the decade. He led the league in steals as a rookie in 1956 and continued to do so for eight more years. His double-play partner, the veteran Nellie Fox, sprayed the ball through the openings Aparicio created and moved him along for the team's RBI men. Fox and Aparicio finished first in just about all the defensive categories, and the rest of the team delivered clutch hits and made big defensive plays on a daily basis. The team's star pitcher was Early Wynn, who was still brushing back hitters at the age of 39. Turk Lown and Gerry Staley, who were nearly as old, served as closers, and Bob Shaw, a career reliever, went 18–6 in a starting role.

The 1959 White Sox did not change

anyone's mind about how to go about building a winning ball club. But they did open a lot of eyes. A carefully constructed pitching staff could out-perform a rotation featuring a couple of big stars. And an offense willing to do something besides sit back and wait for homers could steal itself a lot of runs. It gave the game some very viable options to think about for the 1960s, and it opened the door to a lot of players who might not have made it had they come up during the 1950s.

The Sixties

The 1960s started off with a bang and ended with a whimper. The Yankees returned to the top of the AL standings in 1960, while the Pittsburgh Pirates built up a comfortable lead over their NL opponents and made it hold up all season long. In a bizarre World Series, New York clobbered the Pirates 16-3, 10-0, and 12-0, but dropped games one, four, and five by a total of six runs. Game seven was a dramatic seesaw affair that went into the bottom of the ninth tied 9-9. Bill Mazeroski, Pittsburgh's light-hitting second baseman, led off the inning with a home run, and the Pirates were suddenly and quite unexpectedly world champions.

With no dominant team in the National League, Pittsburgh had won the pennant with consistent pitching from veterans Bob Friend and Vernon Law, good defense up the middle, and a terrific season from Dick Groat. A tremendous natural athlete, Groat was a former All-American basketball star at Duke University and even played a season for the Pistons in the NBA. Groat batted .325 in 1960 to lead the league. Since no one had a big hitting or pitching year in the NL, the bulk of the MVP votes went to Groat, who earned high praise from players and managers as the "glue" of the Pirates. Mazeroski also drew plenty of attention, even before his legendary home run. "Maz" was the best defensive second baseman in baseball history. He had it all—soft hands, fancy footwork, a strong arm, and wonderful anticipation. He also turned the double play better than anyone before or since. Another important contributor to the Pirates was 25-year-old Roberto Clemente. He was still a year away from fulfilling his immense potential but managed a .314 average and a team-high 94 RBIs in 1960. Over the next 11 seasons, Clemente won four batting titles and hit .320 or better eight times. He was unorthodox at the plate, often hitting the ball while lunging on his front foot. But his live bat made up for any imperfections, rocketing singles, doubles, and triples to all fields. Clemente could hit any pitch, and when he caught one just right, he had enough power to reach the seats. On defense, he had no equal.

The Yankees, in their return to the top, retooled their lineup with a group of talented young players, including second baseman Bobby Richardson, shortstop Tony Kubek, third baseman Clete Boyer, and rightfielder Roger Maris. The addition of Maris, who was acquired from the Athletics for a package of over-the-hill veterans, was a stroke of genius. In 1960, he hit 39 home runs and led the American League in RBIs and slugging average to win the Most Valuable Player award. The final footnote on the 1960 season was New York's release of Casey Stengel, who the team felt was getting too old. Casey's comment on his unceremonious dumping? He vowed he would never make the mistake of "turning 70" again.

Expansion

In 1961, the major leagues began to expand for the first time since the formation of the American League. The AL added Los Angeles and Minneapolis-St. Paul to its eight teams, and the NL awarded franchises to Houston and New York for the 1962 season. Actually, the Minnesota Twins were not new. The Washington Senators agreed to move there, and a brand new team called the Senators replaced them in Washington, D.C. The expansion clubs were stocked in a draft of unwanted players from the other clubs. It was not terribly fair, and the teams that emerged were not terribly good.

The effect of expansion on the game was remarkable. The level of pitching in baseball was already thin going into the 1960s, in part because football and basketball had begun to attract more of America's big, athletic kids, meaning a percentage of future pitchers were being siphoned off into these other sports—both of which held more promise for college scholarships than baseball. Add to this trend four new pitching staffs, and it meant that there were at least 50 to 60 hurlers in the game who under normal circumstances would have been in the minors.

In 1961, AL hitters went wild, bashing 450 more home runs and scoring almost 2,000 more runs than the year before. Mantle and Maris went on a homer binge that put them both within Babe Ruth's record of 60 with a month to go. Mantle went down in September with an injury and finished with 54. Maris, however, kept on going and ended up with 61, although much was made of the fact that Ruth had set his record during a 154-game schedule while Maris had the benefit of 162 games.

Yankee teammates Roger Maris and Mickey Mantle made a run at Ruth's single-season home-run record in 1961. Maris broke the Babe's mark with 61 dingers.

Expansion produced similar results in the National League in 1962, although not quite so dramatic. The veteran hitters had a field day, with Willie Mays, Hank Aaron, Ernie Banks, and Frank Robinson all in the hunt for the home-run title. In terms of young players having breakthrough seasons, however, the lack of pitching expressed itself in a different way. This could be seen most clearly on the Los Angeles Dodgers, where a group of prospects with very diverse skills all matured at the same time. The team's huge slugger, rightfielder Frank Howard, had been coming along nicely in 1960 and 1961. In 1962 he exploded, belting 31 home runs and collecting

119 RBIs. Center fielder Willie Davis—a .254 hitter in 1961 when he took over for aging Duke Snider—blossomed into a five-category player. The third Dodgers outfielder, Tommy Davis, really caught fire in 1962. He led the NL with 230 hits, 153 RBIs, and a .346 batting average. The most startling performance of the year was turned in by shortstop Maury Wills. The team's leadoff hitter had paced the NL in steals in 1960 and 1961, but in 1962 he lit out for second almost every time he reached first. Wills finished with 104 stolen bases, shattering Ty Cobb's modern record of 96 and propelling the Dodgers to the top of the standings. There were at least 25 pitchers in the National League that year who had no business being on a major-league mound, and Wills took them to the cleaners. And obviously, he ran wild on the veterans, too.

The 1962 National League pennant race ended in a flat-footed tie, with the San Francisco Giants and the Dodgers squaring off in a best-of-three playoff. The Giants won with four runs in the ninth inning of the third game and nearly toppled the Yankees in the World Series. Willie Mays was still the team's big star and would remain so throughout the decade. But he was now surrounded in the lineup by a couple of monster players. Orlando Cepeda had joined the club in 1958 and immediately established himself as a .300 hitter with longball power. In 1961, "The Baby Bull" led the league with 46 home runs and 142 RBIs, splitting the season between the outfield and first base. The team's other outfielder–first baseman was Willie McCovey, who came up late in 1959 and hit .354 to win Rookie of the Year honors. The Giants spotted the big lefty against right-handed pitchers for his first four seasons, then they let him hit against everyone. McCovey played so well the team eventually decided to trade Cepeda.

Pitchers Gain the Upper Hand

Following the 1962 season, a decision was made in the commissioner's office to clarify the rule governing the strike zone. Home runs were coming too easily, and it was believed an intelligent remedy would be to give the pitchers an extra inch or two to work with. The umpires were told that, beginning in 1963, any pitch that crossed the plate between the bottom of the knees and the shoulders should be called a strike. For years, the umps had been calling strikes between the top of the knees and the letters, so the change was not insignificant. This became clear a couple of months into the 1963 season. Home runs had indeed been reduced slightly, but an unintended result of the enlarged strike zone was that batting averages were plummeting and strikeouts were skyrocketing. National League offenses were particularly hard-hit, as team averages dropped by more than 15 points.

For the next six seasons, baseball became a pitcher's game again. In 1963, for instance, not a single American Leaguer topped 100 runs, and only four players batted over .300. In 1965, only one American Leaguer hit more than 30 home runs, and no one in all of baseball had an on-base percentage above .400. The situation got completely out of hand in 1968. In the National League, a player hitting .336 with 37 home runs and 106 RBIs would have won the Triple Crown; in the American League, a .302 average would have won the batting title.

Two-time Cy Young Award–winner
Bob Gibson led the Cardinals to
World Series championships in 1964
and 1967.

Dodger lefthander Sandy Koufax
holds up four baseballs marked with
zeroes, after twirling his fourth
career no-hitter in 1965.

As one might imagine, a premium was placed on hard throwers, who were greatly favored by the new strike zone. Many of the pitches that would have "just missed" in the 1950s and early 1960s, were now unhittable strikes. This helped marginal major leaguers find a niche in the game, but the biggest effect was that a lot of good young pitchers started putting up Hall of Fame numbers. For example, Bob Gibson of the Cardinals was 27 when the rule changed, and he went from being a .500 pitcher to becoming the fiercest competitor in baseball. He proceeded to win 18 or more games in eight of the next 10 seasons, and in 1968 he pitched the Cardinals to their second straight pennant with 13 shutouts and a mi-

croscopic 1.12 ERA. Gibson came at hitters with everything he had. He was baseball's great intimidator and the best big-game pitcher of the 1960s. In three World Series, he won seven straight games, including a pair of Game Sevens, in 1964 and 1967.

The hardest thrower of all in the NL was Sandy Koufax, and he was helped immensely by the rule change. Signed by Brooklyn in 1955, he had always been able to propel the ball 100 mph, but he struggled for years with his control. During a 1961 spring training bus ride, catcher Norm Sherry suggested Koufax throw the ball a little slower and see what happened. The idea worked, and Koufax became the NL strikeout champion. In 1963, however, he truly came into his own, winning 25 games, throwing 11 shutouts and fanning 306 batters. That fall, Koufax beat the Yankees in games one and four to give the Dodgers a spectacular World Series sweep. Over the next three seasons he established himself as the best pitcher in baseball. He won 26 games in 1965 and chalked up 382 strikeouts, which is still a modern record for left-handers. In 1966, he won 27 and struck out more than 300 batters again. Sadly, the 31-year-old Koufax had to retire after the season because of an arthritic elbow.

For pitchers who had already established themselves, the larger strike zone just made them tougher. Koufax's right-handed counterpart on the Dodgers, Don Drysdale, had already led the NL in strikeouts, wins, and shutouts by 1963. His whiplike motion and willingness to move hitters off the plate were only enhanced by the new rule. He and Koufax pitched the Dodgers to the pennant in 1963, 1965, and 1966. After Koufax retired, the Dodgers fell out of contention but not because of Drysdale. In 1968, he pitched through a painful shoulder injury to record six consecutive shutouts.

Another established hurler who found 1963 to his liking was Juan Marichal, the best pitcher ever produced by the Dominican Republic. Able to deliver a wide range of pitches from behind an exaggerated leg kick, Marichal posted an 18–11 mark in 1962 to help the Giants win the pennant. From 1963 to 1969, his numbers got even better: in six of those seven seasons he won between 21 and 26 games. The new strike zone made Marichal almost unhittable. When he was not using his 90 mph fastball, he threw a curve, slider, and screwball—all of which broke downward into that couple of extra inches pitchers had to play with.

In the American League, the pitching was just as good, although there were fewer dominant individuals. The Tigers might have formed a dynasty had they not traded Jim Bunning to the Phillies in 1964, because youngsters Mickey Lolich and Denny McLain developed into the best one-two punch in the league. Lolich's ball moved a lot, and judging by the number of walks he allowed, it is safe to say that he might not have succeeded had he pitched in the 1950s. But he was in the right place at the right time and took full advantage of the enlarged strike zone. In 1967, he led the league in shutouts. In 1968, he went 17–9 during the regular season and then won three games in the World Series. Prior to the fall classic, the 1968 season belonged to McLain. That year everything clicked for the flamboyant right-hander. He pitched 336 innings, struck out 280 batters, and won a remarkable 31 games to earn the MVP award. From 1965 to 1969, McLain averaged 21 wins and four shutouts a year. He was caught gambling on baseball in 1970 and received a suspension. He then returned out of shape and never regained his form. He pitched his last game for the Braves in 1972 then slipped into oblivion.

Another tragic decline was that of Cleveland left-hander Sam McDowell, who managed to control his blazing fastball but could not control a drinking problem that ruined one of the most promising pitching careers in history. From 1965 to 1970, McDowell led the American League in strikeouts five times. He was close to unhittable during the 1960s, often limiting opponents to batting averages under .190. By the age of 28, however, McDowell's drinking was out of control. After three teams tried to turn him around, he left baseball at the age of 32.

THE DRAFT

For the first century of professional baseball, the distribution of young talent was relatively unstructured. When a young player caught the eye of a major-league scout, he usually signed with that team. Occasionally, more than one team expressed interest in the same player, and the player usually went to the highest bidder or the club that had the best reputation. This put the poorer, less successful clubs at a disadvantage. A remedy was devised in the form of the "bonus baby" rule, which stated that a team had to keep a player on its major league roster for two years if he received a large signing bonus. This did little to prevent powerful teams like the Yankees from scooping up good young players (they just let other teams develop them), and it damaged the careers of some great high school prospects, who were thrown into the majors far too early.

In 1964, a bidding war over college star Rick Reichardt was won by the Los Angeles Angels, with Reichardt collecting a cool quarter million just for signing his first pro contract. That was the last straw. In 1965, an amateur draft was put in place, which gave the highest picks to the lowest teams in the standings. It is a system that quickly put bumbling teams such as the Athletics and Mets on an even playing field with baseball's traditional powerhouses and eventually led to unprecedented parity throughout the major leagues.

The first player drafted in 1965 was college outfielder Rick Monday, who went on to have a wonderful career. He was selected by the A's, who could never have landed the Arizona State All-American under the old system. Among the other top prospects going to mediocre teams that year were catcher Ray Fosse (Indians), Joe Coleman (Senators), and Jim Spencer (Angels). Signing bonuses during the early years of the draft averaged around $25,000 for first-round picks, with a few players topping the $100,000 mark. Today, Reichardt's $250,000 seems like a bargain, as bonuses for first-round picks, such as J. D. Drew, have escalated into the millions.

High-Flying Birds

The classic team of the 1960s was the St. Louis Cardinals. From 1964 to 1969, the Cardinals won three pennants with clutch pitching, excellent defense, speed on the bases, and production at the plate. Besides Gibson, the constants over the years were Lou Brock, Curt Flood, and Tim McCarver. Brock was an aggressive hitter and base runner who spent a good deal of his time in scoring position for the big hitters who passed through the organization, like Ken Boyer, Bill White, Orlando Cepeda, and Roger Maris. When World Series time came around, Brock turned his performance up

Lefthander Sam McDowell was one of the most feared pitchers in the 1960s.

Outfielder Curt Flood waged a courageous battle against the reserve clause. Although his suit against Major League Baseball was unsuccessful, it set the stage for free agency.

another notch, hitting homers, stealing bases, and driving opposing pitchers crazy. He was not much of a leftfielder, but he did not have to be, for patrolling center for the Cards was Flood, one of the best defensive outfielders ever. Flood could also handle himself at the plate, leading the league in hits in 1964 and batting over .300 six times during his 12 years in St. Louis. McCarver was a smart, creative catcher who could handle a pitching staff as well as a bat. He took over as the regular backstop in 1963 and started 100-plus games every year through the end of the decade. The Cardinals won because they specifically did not rely upon a core group of sluggers to do their damage. They had some power hitters come through their team, but the constants

were the supporting cast, which was the very best in baseball from the mid-1960s on.

Hitting Stars of the 1960s

What little hitting there was in the American League after 1962 was supplied by Carl Yastrzemski, Tony Oliva, and Harmon Killebrew. Yastrzemski, who took over from Ted Williams as Boston's leftfielder, played Fenway Park's Green Monster like a virtuoso and regularly challenged for the batting title. Yaz is most fondly remembered for the power display he put on during the final weeks of the 1967 season, when he won the Triple Crown and led the

Red Sox past the Tigers, Twins, and White Sox in the tightest pennant race in history. Like Yastrzemski, Oliva was also a three-time batting champ. The Twins rightfielder won his first as a rookie in 1963 then repeated in 1964. A free swinger who exhibited exciting natural ability and a real joy for the game, he led the AL in hits five times between 1963 and 1970 and made the All-Star team every single season. A 1971 knee injury all but crippled Oliva, who in his prime seemed a good bet for 3,000 hits and a place in the Hall of Fame. Injuries also hampered fellow Twin Killebrew, but when he was healthy, "Killer" lived up to his nickname, topping the 30 home-run mark eight times during the 1960s and leading the league in round-trippers five times between 1962 and 1969. Killebrew specialized in tape-measure jobs. He once hit a ball completely out of Tiger Stadium, and on another occasion hit one in Minnesota that traveled so far that the two seats shattered by the ball were painted orange and never sold again. The 1969 season turned out to be Killebrew's best, as he hit 49 home runs and drove in 140 runs despite being walked 145 times.

One player who hit well in both league was Frank Robinson. In 1961, he had a monster season to carry the Reds to the pennant. In 1962 he won his third straight slugging title and would have led the league in batting and total bases had the numbers compiled by Tommy Davis and Willie Mays in that year's three-game playoff not counted in the regular-season statistics. Robinson's performance leveled off from 1963 to 1965, as did that of many major leaguers. Cincinnati general manager Bill Dewitt had a hunch that his star was entering the twilight years of his career and

traded him to the Orioles for a couple of pitchers. Robinson responded by leading the American League in runs, home runs, RBIs, batting, slugging, and on-base percentage. He teamed with 1964 MVP Brooks Robinson and young slugger Boog Powell to form the nucleus of a team that went on to win the world championship in 1966 and 109 games in 1969 on the way to another pennant. That 1969 Orioles team might well have been the best of the decade. Its pitching staff featured veteran screwballer Mike Cuellar, a crafty left-hander named Dave McNally, and young Jim Palmer, who bounced back strong from surgery. It had everything: power, speed, defense, and pitching.

The Miracle Mets

The one thing Baltimore did not have on its side was destiny. In 1969, the New York Mets had that market cornered. From laughable beginnings in 1962, the franchise had started collecting young pitchers and mixing veterans into its batting order. The team had never enjoyed anything remotely close to a winning season, but it had a winning manager in Gil Hodges, the former Brooklyn Dodgers first baseman. He allowed his youngsters to make mistakes, but never more than once; he never chewed out his players, instead he counseled and cajoled them. In 1969, a trio of young flamethrowers—Tom Seaver, Jerry Koosman, and Gary Gentry—won 55 games, and the defense played mistake-free ball all year long. It had to, for on paper, the offense was pathetic. New York's only consistent power threat was centerfielder Tommie Agee, who batted leadoff. New York had just one .300 hitter in its everyday lineup, Cleon Jones,

The 1969 Miracle Mets stunned the world with an improbable pennant run. They then shocked the powerful Baltimore Orioles in the World Series.

and no one on the team even came close to knocking in more than 80 runs. Yet, whoever Hodges chose to play seemed to rise to the occasion and get the job done. The Mets won the division by eight games, disposed of the powerful Braves in the first National League Championship Series, then squeezed the life out of the powerful Orioles in one of the great upsets in World Series history. Baltimore fans are still wondering how the anemic Mets won, and Mets fans still talk of 1969 as if they were witness to a little baseball black magic.

The 1960s struck a happy balance between the pitching and "inside baseball" of the Dead Ball era and the lusty hitting that had characterized the sport since then. Unfortunately, they did not blend as seamlessly as they might have. That would happen to a greater degree during the 1970s, when the pitchers lost the advantage they had gained in the 1960s, and teams brought more varied offensive weapons into play. By the end

of the 1960s, organizations no longer searched for a certain type of ballplayer, they simply looked for the best ballplayers they could find. This laid the groundwork for some of the most interesting teams and multitalented players in baseball history— and a decade of unfathomable change for the game.

The 1970s

In the 1950s, team speed was a novelty. In the 1960s it was a fallback strategy when teams were short on hitting. By the 1970s, team speed had become the single most important part of the game. Beginning with the Astrodome in 1965, baseball saw grass slowly replaced by artificial turf, until by the end of the 1970s 10 teams were playing on the plastic stuff. This revolution in playing surfaces was ushered in by a new round of stadium building, and those stadiums tended to be a little less friendly

Opened in 1965, the Houston Astrodome was baseball's first indoor ballpark. The original grass died and was replaced in 1966 with a type of plastic grass known as Astroturf.

to power hitting than the old-time parks. With faster surfaces, longer foul lines, and more room in the power alleys, baseball began looking for hitters who could run and outfielders who could cover a lot of territory. Sluggers were still highly coveted, of course, but the slow-footed .250 hitter who belted 20 homers a year (and during the 1960s every team had one or two) went the way of the dinosaur. As for pitching, in 1969 the strike zone was reduced and the mound lowered, taking back from pitchers the advantage they had enjoyed since 1963.

Baseball in the 1970s offered fans great defense, exciting base running, plenty of .300 hitters, and enough premiere sluggers to keep devotees of the power game very happy. The take-backs in pitching worked pretty well, too. The good pitchers adjusted and thrived, while the marginal ones went back to being marginal. Attendance was way up from the 1960s for three reasons:

most of the new stadiums were built in areas that were accessible to fans in the suburbs; the divisional alignment instituted in 1969 created four pennant races each year instead of two; and baseball was just a lot more fun to watch.

One particular aspect of baseball in the 1970s made it completely different from any other time in its history: the designated hitter rule. In 1973, the American League voted to insert a full-time pinch hitter in the lineup instead of letting the pitcher bat. The idea was to increase offense and to extend the careers of players who could still hit but could no longer play the field. The DH represented the first major difference in playing rules between the two leagues since 1903, and it caused some complications in inter-league play. But everyone got used to it after a while, and life went on. The result, as one might expect, was a slight boost in offense in the AL. Also, fans got a final chance to

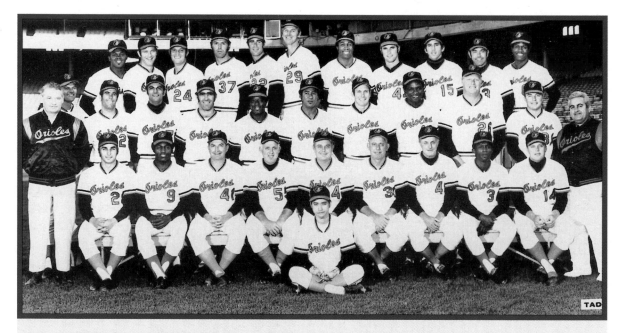

The powerhouse 1971 Baltimore Orioles featured four 20-game winners but fell to the Pittsburgh Pirates in the World Series.

watch some pretty good ballplayers who might otherwise have retired. Former stars Willie McCovey, Orlando Cepeda, Tommy Davis, Willie Horton, Rico Carty, Billy Williams, Deron Johnson, and Harmon Killebrew all squeezed a couple more years out of their aching knees thanks to the DH. Even Hank Aaron, who broke Babe Ruth's all-time home run record with the Braves in 1974, played two extra years with the Milwaukee Brewers thanks to the new rule. A result of the DH rule that was not good, however, was the lengthening of games. Because AL managers did not have to worry about pinch hitting for their pitchers anymore, they could use more relievers in close ballgames. The extra trips to the mound, and the extra time allotted for warming up new pitchers remains a problem to this day.

The O's

In the American League, the Baltimore Orioles continued to field strong teams throughout the decade, winning five Eastern Division titles and reaching the World Series in 1970, 1971, and 1979. The Orioles used the same formula that had been successful for them in the 1960s: defense, pitching, and home runs. On defense, Paul Blair was the best centerfielder in the league; Brooks Robinson the best third baseman; and Mark Belanger the best shortstop. The trio of Palmer, Cuellar, and Mc-Nally was joined by curveball artist Pat Dobson, and in 1971 each reached the 20-win plateau. And everyone chipped in in the power department, with first baseman Boog Powell leading the way. The Orioles faded when their veterans began to lose a step, and manager Earl Weaver was slow to incorporate the running game into his attack. By the end of the decade, however, Baltimore was back on top with a more balanced lineup that featured speedy outfielders, a creative platoon system, and a young switch-hitter named Eddie Murray, whose clutch hitting put the Orioles back into contention for the division crown. The one constant for Baltimore throughout the decade was the fine pitching of Palmer. He was the league's most consistent winner, recording 20 or more victories eight times during the 1970s. Only one AL right-hander in history, Walter Johnson, ever had more. Palmer's best year was 1975, when he led the Orioles to the playoffs with 23 wins, 10 shutouts, and a league-best 2.09 ERA. That season brought Palmer the second of his three Cy Young awards.

The A's

The most entertaining team in the league was the Oakland A's, who won the Western Division crown from 1971 to 1975 and captured three straight world championships beginning in 1972. The team had great pitching, tremendous speed, and baseball's most dynamic slugger. They also exhibited tremendous unity (a rare thing in the "Me" decade) thanks to their singular hatred for Charles Finley, a cheap, meddling owner who tried any gimmick he could think of to draw a few extra fans into the park. For all his shortcomings, however, the Oakland boss did put great talent on the field. The left side of the infield featured third baseman Sal Bando, a fine fielder and one of the game's toughest hitters with men in scoring position, and shortstop Bert Campaneris, the league's premier base-stealing threat. This combination alone would have given the A's a productive lineup, but the team had one of the best all-around leftfielders in the game in Joe Rudi, a lightning-fast centerfielder in Billy North, and a collection of home-run hitters who rotated in and out of the first base and designated hitter slots. And then, on top of all that, there was Reggie Jackson.

Rookie Reggie Jackson shows his batting stance in this 1968 photograph. Jackson smashed 563 home runs in his 21-year career.

Jackson possessed supreme power with an ego to match. He loved to be the center of attention, both on the field and off, and showed a special flair for coming up with dramatic hits in dramatic situations. During his years with the A's, Jackson enjoyed Ruthian hot streaks and historical slumps, and it would be quite accurate to say that there was rarely a dull moment when he was around. The bottom line, however, is that he was a tremendously productive all-around player. Jackson held his own in rightfield, he ran the bases with good speed and great cunning, he clouted monstrous home runs, and outside of Oakland's County Stadium—a bad ball park for hitters—he hit for a high average. From 1969 to 1975, Reggie led the league in runs, home runs, and slugging average twice, and he won the 1973 MVP award.

The Oakland starting staff was a good one. Left-hander Vida Blue made it to the majors at age 20 and threw a no-hitter in his first season. In his second year, he went 24–8 with a 1.82 ERA to win both the Cy Young award and the MVP. The star right-hander for the A's was Jim "Catfish" Hunter. Although he had a good fastball and could get a strikeout when he needed it, he preferred to let his fielders do the work. Hunter led the American League in winning percentage in 1972 and 1973 and posted a league-high 25 wins in 1974. In 1975, Hunter became baseball's first "free agent" after Finley tried to get out of paying into a life insurance fund that had been part of his 1974 contract. Hunter claimed that the owner had violated his contract, and therefore he was free to negotiate with any team he wished; arbitrator Peter Seitz agreed, and Hunter signed a $3.5-million deal to pitch for the Yankees. His salary with the A's had been $100,000.

Hunter, Blue, and the other Oakland starters had the great luxury of relying upon the game's best bullpen to clean up after them. They knew that if they could keep the team in the game for six innings, a win was practically guaranteed. Bob Locker, Darold Knowles, Paul Lindblad, and Horacio Pina shut down hitters in the middle innings, then the ball went to Rollie Fingers, the first player to truly make a science of relief pitching. Fingers had excellent control but never possessed overpowering stuff. Yet he had a great knowledge of hitters and what their tendencies were in late-inning situations. He could actually pitch to a batter's weakness without the batter even realizing it.

Free Agency

The Catfish Hunter deal made other baseball stars realize how much money was really out there for them, and the players began to push hard to create a freer market. Dave McNally and Andy Messersmith—two of the best pitchers in baseball—played the 1975 season without signing contracts, and their clubs simply exercised the standard one-year option and paid them their 1974 salaries, as outlined in the reserve clause. At year's end, however, Messersmith and McNally insisted that they had fulfilled their contractual commitments, and therefore their teams no longer had any claim on them. It all came down to the wording of the clause, much of which dated back to the 19th century, when government tended to side with big business on labor issues. Arbitrator Seitz, back on the case, agreed with the players and declared that McNally, Messersmith, and anyone else who chose to play out their option should be free to negotiate with any teams they chose.

Seitz's ruling touched off total panic among the owners. If players chose not to sign their 1976 contracts, and the teams automatically renewed them, then every player in baseball would be free to sell his services to the highest bidder in 1977. The players were thrilled to have conquered the owners, but they realized that this scenario would create a lot of chaos, too. So when the 1976 season concluded, the owners and players hammered out an agreement on "free agency" that would reshape the game. In all, 20 players tested the free agent waters in 1977. By far the biggest was Reggie Jackson, who signed with the New York Yankees.

The Straw That Stirred the Drink

The Yankees ballclub was already a good one, having captured the 1976 pennant, but a four-game sweep by the power-laden Reds embarrassed owner George Steinbrenner, who shelled out millions for Jackson and Cincinnati ace Don Gullett. Jackson had once said that if he played in New York, they would name a candy bar after him. Prior to spring training in 1977, he predicted that he would be the straw that stirred the Yankee drink. Both comments proved prophetic. Jackson was showered with REG-GIE! bars after hitting a home run in the Yankee home opener and provided a much-needed long-ball threat as the team went on to win the pennant.

The team put on the field by the New York Yankees between 1976 and 1978 was one of the toughest collection of ballplayers ever assembled. Despite a constant media circus surrounding the club, they were a smart, focused group that did everything well. Graig Nettles teamed with Jackson to give the Yanks baseball's best lefthanded power tandem, and he succeeded Brooks Robinson as the best big-game third baseman in the league. At the top of the lineup, centerfielder Mickey Rivers provided speed and clutch hitting; at the bottom Bucky Dent supplied sure hands at short-

The 1977 Yankees won the first of two consecutive World Series championships. Through free agency, the team was able to put an All-Star at every position.

This 1970 trading card pictures home-run king Hank Aaron, who broke Ruth's career home-run record in 1974 and finished with 755 lifetime round-trippers.

hurler in history. Guidry went 25–3 with 248 strikeouts and a 1.74 ERA, leading the AL in all three categories. Ed Figueroa, the number two man on the staff, won 55 games from 1976 to 1978; only a rainout on the final day of the 1976 season kept him from becoming the first Puerto Rican to win 20 games in a season. In 1978, "Figgy" did win 20, and the Yankees needed every one of those victories to catch the Red Sox. The two clubs ended the year tied with 99 wins, forcing a one-game playoff, which the Yanks won on a dramatic three-run homer by Dent.

Sox Woes

It was not the first time during the 1970s that the Red Sox had come to the brink of success and then fallen agonizingly short. In 1972, they blew the division title to an ancient Detroit team led by 37-year-old Al Kaline. And in 1975, the Red Sox made it all the way to the World Series but lost to the Reds in seven games. They could take some solace in that the 1975 World Series ranked among the most exciting and well-played of all time, especially the sixth game, a wild see-saw affair won by Carlton Fisk with a home run in the 12th inning. Fisk, who rivaled Munson as the AL's top catcher during the 1970s, was the key player on the Red Sox, along with veteran Carl Yastrzemski. These two were joined in 1975 by Jim Rice and Fred Lynn, perhaps the best rookie duo any team ever had. Rice was an aggressive right-handed hitter with quick wrists, lightning reflexes, and a rock-hard physique. When he hit the ball, it made the kind of noise Hank Aaron had produced during his prime years with the Braves. Lynn, a left-handed hitter, had the

stop and surprising pop. In the middle of the lineup, Jackson and Nettles were joined by first baseman Chris Chambliss—a model of consistency in the field and at the plate—and Thurman Munson, who gave the team grit, character, and a .300-hitting catcher who could drive in 100 runs a season.

The highly paid Hunter was hurt on Opening Day in 1977 and never regained his previous form, but he was replaced as staff ace by Ron Guidry. The slightly built left-hander set up hitters with a live fastball then punched them out with a hard-biting slider. He was magnificent down the stretch in 1977, and in 1978 he was as good as any kind of year no one believed possible from a rookie. He finished second in the league with a .331 average and was tops in runs, doubles, and slugging. Lynn made game-saving catches and clutch hits all season long; when all was said and done, he was not only Rookie of the Year but also American League MVP.

The Big Red Machine

In the NL, the team to beat most years was the Cincinnati Reds. From 1970 to 1978, the Reds were managed by Sparky Anderson, an upbeat young skipper who understood better than anyone how to blend power and speed for the best results on artificial turf. His teams could play you a dozen games and beat you a dozen different ways. As far as pitching was concerned, Anderson never had much to speak of, but he managed his staff with great decisiveness and creativ-

ity. Starting pitchers hated him, because he would pull them at the first hint of trouble. Indeed, Sparky was so notorious for yanking pitchers early that his nickname was Captain Hook. After winning the 1970 pennant, the Big Red Machine sputtered in 1971, prompting a trade of slugging first baseman Lee May to Houston for second baseman Joe Morgan.

Morgan sparked the club's offense for the remainder of the decade, as the Reds won the Western Division title five more times and added three more pennants. He was the league's most patient number-two hitter, drawing 100-plus walks six years in a row, and he was also one of the game's top base stealers. In both 1975 and 1976, Morgan batted over .320, stole more than 60 bases, and led the league in on-base percentage as the Reds won back-to-back world championships. "Little Joe" was selected as the NL MVP both years. Batting ahead of Morgan was Pete Rose, who

The 1976 Reds repeated the accomplishment of the 1975 squad, winning the World Series with a four-game sweep of the New York Yankees.

already had a pair of batting titles under his belt from the late 1960s. Nicknamed "Charlie Hustle" for his aggressive play, Rose was not considered a championship-caliber player until the 1970s, when he became the game's ultimate leadoff hitter. Although he was reaching base at roughly the same rate as always, he had become next-to-impossible to get out when it really mattered. Pitchers had been setting up hitters to go after "their pitch" for a century, but Rose turned the tables, setting up pitchers so that they often gave him "his pitch." Rose's focus and durability enabled him to produce 200-hit seasons well into his 30s, and this in turn enabled him to join the 3,000-hit club. In fact, by the time he retired as an active player at the age of 45, Rose had become the club's most prolific member with 4,256 hits. Rose was shifted from the outfield to third when George Foster emerged as an everyday player in 1975. A dead pull-hitter with quick wrists, massive shoulders, and a wasp-thin waist, Foster was the league's most feared RBI man with Rose and Morgan hitting ahead of him. Add to this mix Tony Perez, a powerful, clutch-hitting first baseman, and pitchers had an awful lot to worry about when facing the Reds.

What made Cincinnati the decade's dominant team, however, was its catcher, Johnny Bench. Bench became the first-string backstop in 1968 at the age of 20, and even as a rookie he was doing things that would ultimately revolutionize the position. Catchers had long been taught to catch with two hands; Bench was so quick and coordinated that he could catch with one. The advantages of this style were numerous. With his right hand behind his back instead of next to his mitt, Bench did not run the risk

of getting his fingers smashed by a foul tip. It also left him in a better position to release the ball quickly on throws to second base, which was critical given the number of base stealers in the National League. And because he could catch with one hand, it meant he did not have to throw his body in front of as many errant pitches; he just flicked his glove at the ball and there it was. The biggest advantage of this style was that it reduced the wear and tear on Bench, enabling him to stay in the lineup for 140 to 150 games a year—at the time an unprecedented amount for a catcher. That was very important, because Bench could really hit. In 1970, he blasted 45 homers and knocked in 148 runs to win the National League MVP. In 1972, he led the league in home runs and RBIs again, winning his second MVP. And in 1974, he led the league in RBIs a third time, while scoring 108 runs. In 13 years as a regular behind the plate, Bench collected 10 Gold Gloves and established more than a dozen offensive records for the position.

Hitting Stars of the 1970s

Besides Bench, the National League's premiere sluggers during the 1970s were Willie Stargell and Mike Schmidt. Stargell, who played his entire career with the Pittsburgh Pirates, spent many of his prime years in Forbes Field, one of the toughest parks for home-run hitters. When the team moved into symmetrical Three Rivers Stadium, Stargell strung together some great years, including 1973, when he produced the exceedingly difficult combination of 43 doubles and 44 homers and led the league in RBIs. In 1979, at the age of 39, "Pops" ignited an amazing September charge by the Pirates, depriving the Expos of what looked like a sure division title. Schmidt, one of the best "guess" hitters in history, guessed correctly often enough during the 1970s to lead the league in home runs three times. An undisciplined swinger with a so-so glove when he won the starting third base job for the Philadelphia Phillies in 1973, Schmidt increased his walks and cut down on his strikeouts and became a Gold Glover. His best offensive seasons actually came during the early 1980s, as he remained one of baseball's top offensive players from 1974 to 1987. When Schmidt broke into the majors, a great debate surrounded the issue of baseball's best-ever third sacker. When he retired, the question was as good as settled—no one else comes close to Schmidt's all-around excellence.

The decade of multiple skills produced a great many multiskilled players. In the National League, Dave Parker of the Pirates combined power, speed, high average, and great defense in a scintillating package, as did Cesar Cedeno of the Astros. Sadly, both men saw their careers sidetracked—Parker by drug addiction and Cedeno by stress problems following the accidental shooting of his girlfriend. Infielder Bill Madlock of the Cubs won batting titles in 1975 and 1976, then joined the Pirates at mid-season in 1979 to help them win the pennant. He stayed with the club for seven years and won two more batting crowns in the 1980s. Catcher Ted Simmons of the Cardinals had the misfortune of playing at the same time as Bench but distinguished himself with six .300 seasons between 1971 and 1980. His teammate, Lou Brock, continued to refine his game and led the league in stolen bases

Willie Stargell awaits a pitch. The Pirates slugger led his team to the 1979 World Series championship.

four times in a row. In 1974, he broke the record set in 1962 by Maury Wills when modern swiped 118 bases. Brock retired after the 1979 season with more than 3,000 hits and 900 steals. The Dodgers had a quartet of good all-around players in first baseman Steve Garvey, second baseman Davey Lopes, and outfielders Reggie Smith and Dusty Baker. Garvey won the MVP in 1974 with 200 hits and 111 RBIs, and Lopes chipped in with 10 homers and 59 steals to help the Dodgers win the pennant. These two were joined by Smith, Baker, and third baseman Ron Cey to form the nucleus of the Los Angeles pennant-winners in 1977 and 1978.

In the American League, Rod Carew of the Twins won seven batting championships between 1969 and 1978. An intelligent hitter who adjusted his stance and swing depending on the count and the pitcher he was facing, Carew put so much top-spin on the ball that infielders rarely got to his grounders unless they were hit within a few feet of them. He was fast, too, stealing 35-plus bases four years in a row. Never more than an average defensive player, Carew moved from second base to first base in 1976 and kept right on hitting. In 1978 he had a wonderful year, leading the AL in runs, hits, triples, batting, and on-base percentage. Edging Carew for the hitting crown in 1976 was third baseman George Brett of the Kansas City Royals. Brett's batting championship was the first of three he would win during 20 seasons as a regular. A lethal offensive player who hit the ball where it was pitched, he sprayed singles, doubles, and triples to all fields but could also hit a home run if a pitcher tried to sneak the ball over the inside part of the plate.

Pitching Stars of the 1970s

The American League also had a couple of baseball's most interesting pitchers during the 1970s. Gaylord Perry came to the Indians from the Giants in 1972 in a trade for Sam McDowell. He had topped the NL in wins in 1970, but the Giants believed he was on the downside of his career; they saw in McDowell a chance to get a guy with a lot of wins left in his arm. For once, the Indians lucked out. While McDowell drank his way out of baseball, Perry blossomed in his new situation, winning 64 games over the next three seasons. Perry, who admitted to throwing a spitball, returned to the National League in 1978 with the Padres to win 21 games at the age of 40 and then hung on for five more years to finish with 314 career victories. Another ageless wonder was Luis Tiant, who first achieved fame with the Indians when he led the AL in shutouts in 1966 and 1968. He would twist around until his back faced home plate, lift his leg high in the air, release the ball anywhere from over-the-top to submarine style, and in general make life miserable for opposing batters. A broken shoulder all but ended Tiant's career in 1970, and a comeback attempt in 1971 with the Red Sox was a disaster. But Boston hung on to Tiant and their patience paid off, as he won 96 games over the next five seasons and pitched them to division titles in 1972 and 1975.

The most impressive pitcher in the American League during the 1970s was Nolan Ryan. Traded by the Mets to the Angels in 1972, he finally got his 100 mph fastball under control and immediately became history's most awesome strikeout artist. During his first six years in the AL,

Ryan struck out more than 300 batters an unprecedented five times, including a record 383 in 1973. Despite playing for a lousy team, he managed to win more than 16 games six times during the decade, with a high of 22 in 1974. No one could touch Ryan when he was on; he held the American League to a sub-.200 average four times. Some have wondered what he might have done had he pitched from 1963 to 1968. Others simply marveled that he was still throwing in the high-90s during the 1990s. By the time Ryan retired at the age of 46, he had won 324 games, struck out a record 5,714 batters, and had seven no-hitters to his credit.

Steve Carlton and Tom Seaver, the two best pitchers in the National League during the 1970s, had pretty good fastballs of their own. Carlton mixed his with history's best slider, and the result was four 20-win seasons during the decade. After going 20-9 for the 1971 Cardinals, he was shipped to the Phillies, where he won the Cy Young award despite playing for a last-place ball club. Over the next few seasons, a team of erratic youngsters grew up around "Lefty," and by the end of the decade the Phillies were one of the NL's top teams. A fitness and stretching devotee, Carlton stayed at the top of his game until his late 30s and pitched in the big leagues until he was 43. In all, he led the NL in wins four times, strikeouts five times, and won the Cy Young on four occasions during his 24-year career. Seaver had the good luck of maturing during the Mets' phenomenal 1969 season and the bad luck of being a Met throughout most of the 1970s. For many of those years, he was the lone bright spot for New York, adding two more Cy Young awards to the one he received in 1969. Seaver's near-perfect me-

Fireballer Nolan Ryan retired in 1993 with 324 wins and two impressive records: seven career no-hitters and 5,714 career strikeouts.

chanics enabled him to throw a lot of innings and kept him in the game for 20 years. He led the National League in strikeouts five times between 1970 and 1976, and he was the ERA champion three times in four seasons beginning in 1970. A 1977 trade to Cincinnati broke his heart, but the Mets were on the verge of collapse and the Reds were a pennant contender, so he said a tearful goodbye and proceeded to win 21 games and lead the league in shutouts. Seaver continued to pitch well for eight more seasons, finishing his career with 311 wins and 3,640 strikeouts.

By 1979, baseball was healthy and wealthy. Free agency had not destroyed the game, as many owners feared. Instead, it created publicity for baseball each winter, excitement each spring, and realistic hope for teams that needed that one extra player to become a contender. Attendance during the decade skyrocketed, growing from just under 29 million in 1970 to more than 43 million in 1979. Two new franchises—the Toronto Blue Jays and Seattle Mariners—were added in 1977, and in 1979 there was an exciting crop of young stars getting their first taste of the big leagues, including Rickey Henderson, Kirk Gibson, and Tim Raines. Some said it would take a major blunder on baseball's part to mess up this situation. Others said it was just too good to be true.

The 1980s

The 1980s began with great promise for baseball. The decade's first World Series, between the Kansas City Royals and the Philadelphia Phillies, turned out to be a real milestone for the game. The Royals were the first of the 1969 expansion teams to win the pennant, while the Phillies were the last of the original 16 major-league franchises from 1901 to win a world championship. On the field, the game did indeed fulfill the promise of that first season. Throughout the decade, the pennant was up for grabs almost every year, which meant that new teams and new stars were constantly being thrust into the spotlight. Rookies were a big story during the 1980s. With salaries for veterans escalating, many owners handed everyday jobs to first-year players, creating more opportunities for the game's young studs. Some blossomed, and some fell flat on their faces, but their stories created great excitement and anticipation among the fans every year. The 1980s also belonged to the old. With big bucks as an incentive, many veterans who in days past would have quit the game stayed in great shape and remained productive into their late 30s and even into their 40s.

Strike One!

Off the field, however, the game was a mess. The players and the owners behaved disgracefully, endlessly antagonizing each other and, far worse, ignoring the fans in the process. The trouble began when the owners attempted to win back some of what they had lost with the advent of free agency five years earlier. They demanded compensation for losing a player to another team, and they proposed that the team signing a top free agent be compelled to give up its 16th-best player in return. The players would not hear of it. They argued that a team knowing it would lose a valuable player would be less likely to bid for a free agent and less likely to offer a fair salary. The owners purchased strike insurance, then told the players they would not budge on this issue. On June 12th, everything came to a grinding halt. For the first time in history, there was no baseball during the summer. The strike lasted seven weeks and one day; when the owners' insurance ran out, they quickly gave in. But a third of the season was lost forever, and there was a hollowness to the rest of the year, including what should have been a great World Series between the Yankees and the Dodgers.

Strike Two!

Several other disasters befell baseball during the 1980s. In 1985, the players and owners (still squabbling over money) reached another impasse, and the players walked off the field on August 2. Most people had forgiven the game for its lost season in 1981, but the moment it looked like 1985 would be a replay, public opinion turned ugly. For the first time in a long

In June 1981, Chicago's Wrigley Field sits empty while baseball players strike. The work stoppage lasted 50 days.

time, the fans were heard and the labor dispute was settled after only two days. But that September, all eyes turned to a highly publicized drug trial in Pittsburgh. As testimony unfolded, it became evident that a lot of baseball players were heavy cocaine users and that drug dealers had infiltrated some major-league clubhouses. The problem seemed to date back to the late 1970s, and some big names were definitely involved. This ended any illusion that baseball was a "clean" game—its wholesome image was completely destroyed.

The owners had had enough. Unable to curb free agency in the courts or at the negotiating table, they secretly agreed amongst themselves that no one would sign another team's best players. Their plan was to leave a player with no choice other than signing with his old team, at whatever salary his old team deemed appropriate. This arrangement was not only unfair, it was illegal. The players knew what was going on, but there was no solid proof that the owners were working in collusion against them. Some of the game's biggest stars shopped their services only to receive offers that came in below what their old teams were offering—or worse, no offers at all. Left with few options, free agents either stayed with their teams or signed with other clubs for a lot less money. Eventually, this plot blew up in the owners' faces.

Somehow, in this atmosphere of greed, overindulgence, and self-destruction, baseball was actually being played, and fans were watching the game in record numbers. Division races usually were tight and highly spirited affairs, and no less than 21 different teams participated in post-season play during the 1980s. The only franchises that fell short were the Seattle Mariners, Cleveland Indians, Texas Rangers, Pittsburgh Pirates, and Cincinnati Reds. But this decade, perhaps more than any previous one, belonged to the players and not the teams.

ANDRE ROLLS THE DICE

The player who finally exposed the collusion conspiracy was Andre Dawson. One of the best all-around performers during the 1980s, he suffered from aching knees and desperately wanted to leave the Montreal Expos, who played on a hard artificial surface. When it was clear that no team other than the Expos wanted to negotiate, he went to the Chicago Cubs. The Cubs were the perfect team for Dawson—they knew it and he knew it. They played on grass, and the dimensions of Wrigley Field were ideal for a right-handed power hitter like Dawson. The Cubs, however, claimed they could not afford him. How could they say that, Dawson wondered? They had not even discussed a salary!

In a rare and often overlooked act of selflessness, Dawson signed a blank contract, handed it to the Cubs and told them to fill in whatever salary they felt they could afford. Incredibly, the Cubs refused. This was a monumental mistake, for it gave the players their first piece of concrete evidence that the owners were acting in collusion. When word got out that the Cubs had turned down a blank contract from one of baseball's best players, the other owners pleaded with Chicago to fill in a number—any number—and take Dawson. They did, but it was too late. The Dawson affair eventually snowballed into a complex court case, and the owners were found guilty of collusion over a three-year period. They had to repay lost wages to the short-changed free agents, plus a huge fine. In the end, their stupid plan had cost them far more than they saved by trying to keep salaries down. Unfortunately, the collusion also ended or negatively altered the careers of many of baseball's finest players.

The collusion episode brought out an interesting paradox that had existed in baseball for a very long time. The game's owners are essentially business partners—the more they work together, the better off they are. Yet the reality is, and always has been, that the owners are constantly competing against one another for players, revenue, media coverage, and anything else they feel has value. The game's players are essentially competitors—the harder they compete against one another, the more likely they are to build up their statistics and win games. Yet the reality is, and always has been, that the players have worked together as well as any organized labor group in the country. They have, time and again, shown a willingness to make sacrifices for each other, and for future players, even if it has a negative impact on what they are trying to accomplish on the field.

The upward spiral in salaries during the free agent era was not caused by the players. It was the owners who engaged in bidding wars that caused their costs to soar and ate into their profits. This fundamental problem caused plenty of unrest during the 1980s. During the 1990s it would do the unthinkable.

Dynamic Duos

In the American League, there were a number of headline-grabbing duos. Infielders Paul Molitor and Robin Yount turned the Milwaukee Brewers into a winning team in 1978, and boosted them into the playoffs for the first time in 1981. In 1982, Yount led the league in hits, doubles and slugging, while Molitor led the league in runs and swiped 41 bases. Yount took the MVP that season, Molitor finished 12th, and Milwaukee sluggers Cecil Cooper and Gorman Thomas placed fifth and eighth, respectively. And the Brewers won their first pennant. Milwaukee's pitching collapsed the following year, leaving the door open for the AL's next pennant-winning tandem, Cal Ripken and Eddie Murray. Ripken made the game look easy in 1982, when he won the Rookie of the Year award. In 1983, the 22-year-old shortstop elevated his game even higher, leading the league in hits, runs, and doubles to win the MVP. Murray, a 27-year-old veteran, had developed into a fearsome power hitter, and his 33 homers were tops among first basemen in 1983. By the time they were through, Yount, Molitor, and Murray each surpassed 3,000 lifetime hits, and Ripken broke Lou Gehrig's mark for consecutive games played.

In Dave Winfield and Don Mattingly, the Yankees offered fans a dynamic duo that went right down to the wire for the American League batting title in 1984. Winfield, who spent his first eight years with the San Diego Padres, came to the Yanks as a free agent in 1981. Winfield maintained a high level of performance during his eight-plus years as a Yankee, knocking in 100 or more runs six times. In 1984, he stopped trying for home runs and shortened up on his

Cal Ripkin awaits his turn at bat. On September 6, 1995, he played in his 2,131st consecutive game to eclipse Lou Gehrig's record.

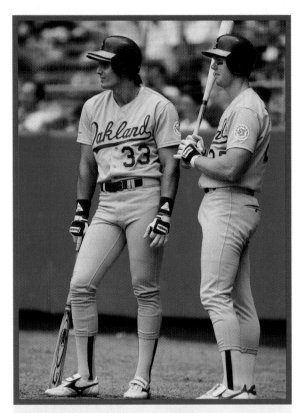

The Bash Brothers—sluggers Jose Canseco and Mark McGwire—led the Oakland Athletics to two World Series titles in the late 1980s.

swing. The result was a 57-point jump in his batting average to .340. Mattingly, a product of New York's farm system, was playing his first full year in 1984, and he led the league in hits, doubles, and batting, as he edged Winfield by three points on the final day of the season. Winfield would reach the 3,000-hit plateau before retiring, while Mattingly's career was cut short by a back injury. While healthy, though, "Donnie Baseball" was the game's most productive player, averaging better than 200 hits, 40 doubles, 25 homers, 110 RBIs, and a .325 batting mark between 1984 and 1989. He also won five Gold Gloves during that stretch.

The decade's final dominant duo was Jose Canseco and Mark McGwire of the Oakland A's. Canseco broke out first, clubbing 33 homers and knocking in 117 runs as the 21-year-old Rookie of the Year in 1986. McGwire won top rookie honors in 1987 with 49 homers and 118 RBIs, while Canseco chipped in with 31 homers and 113 RBIs. The "Bash Brothers" led the A's to three straight pennants beginning in 1988.

Other American League notables were Wade Boggs, Rickey Henderson, and Kirby Puckett. All three captured the imagination of baseball fans, each doing so in his own special way. Boggs, the Boston Red Sox third baseman, took advantage of the unusual dimensions of Fenway Park better than any player in team history. The left-hander banged outside pitches against the Green Monster for doubles, lined fat strikes to the wide open spaces in right centerfield, and yanked inside offerings down the short rightfield line for home runs. An intense and superstitious player who ate chicken before every game, Boggs won five batting titles between 1983 and 1988 and batted below .300 only once during the first 15 years of his career. Henderson, who broke in with the Oakland A's, shattered Lou Brock's record for steals in 1982 when he swiped 130 bases. But he was more than just a speed demon. Henderson had a keen eye at the plate, drawing 117 walks at the age of 21 and leading the league in that category three times during the decade. He also had tremendous power, which meant that pitchers could not simply groove him a pitch when he had worked the count to 3-0 or 3-1. If they did, he made them pay, establishing a new career record for leadoff home runs. Henderson added the all-time record for stolen bases to his credentials in 1991, and he is the only player in history to steal more than 1,000. In short, Henderson established himself as the finest leadoff hitter the game has ever known. Puckett became a beloved player largely because he did not look like a player. He was built like the Pillsbury Doughboy—short, plump, and low to the ground—but he was quick, strong, and remarkably fluid both in the field and at bat. Puckett played centerfield for the Minnesota Twins, a rag-tag team that was never once picked to win its division. Yet behind Puckett's offensive exploits and big plays in the outfield, the Twins managed to reach the World Series twice and win it both times. He led the American League in hits on four occasions, topped the 100-RBI mark three times, and won the batting title once. Sadly, his career ended suddenly in 1996 when he developed glaucoma and could no longer see clearly out of one eye.

Pitching Stars of the 1980s

Facing these great hitters was a task no AL pitcher relished, and only a select few actually flourished during the decade. The three most prominent AL hurlers were Jack Morris, Bret Saberhagen, and Roger Clemens. Morris, the winningest pitcher of the 1980s, was the ace of the Detroit Tigers staff. He challenged hitters with his fastball and then made them look silly with a dipping split-finger pitch that he learned from coach Roger Craig. When Morris was on a hot streak no one was tougher to beat. Saberhagen keyed a resurgence by the Kansas City Royals in the mid-1980s, when he won 10 games as a 20-year-old in 1984 and then won 20 the next season and captured the Cy Young Award. His hopping fastball and ter-

Speedster Rickey Henderson clutches third base as he celebrates his record-breaking 939th career stolen base in 1991.

rific control belied his youth, as did his ability to make big pitches when a game hung in the balance. Saberhagen was active for six seasons during the 1980s and won 92 games despite a shaky supporting cast. Clemens, who battled arm injuries during his first two years with the Red Sox, put it all together in 1986 and went 24–4 with a league-leading 2.48 ERA to win the Cy Young and MVP awards. "The Rocket" mixed a 95 mph heater with a hard-biting slider and a sinker to win 17 or more games seven years in a row. He also led the AL in shutouts five times, ERA four times, and strikeouts three times before leaving the

Roger Clemens strides toward the plate. The righthander has won three Cy Young awards and holds the record for the most strikeouts in a nine-inning game (20).

Red Sox via free agency after the 1996 season. Untouchable when all of his pitches were working, Clemens struck out a record 20 batters in a 1986 game then repeated this amazing feat a full decade later.

More Hitting Stars of the 1980s

The National League had some terrific hitting twosomes of its own during the 1980s. Gary Carter assumed the honor of baseball's best catcher after Johnny Bench's knees gave out, and the Expos backstop held that distinction throughout the decade. A tremendous on-field leader and deadly hitter in the clutch, Carter, like Bench, stayed in great shape and rarely missed more than 20 games a season. After earning All-Star honors six years in a row with Montreal, he was traded to the Mets in 1985. There, Carter was put in charge of baseball's best young pitching staff, and he handled the hurlers beautifully. He also knocked in 100 runs two straight times and was a key part of New York's 1986 world championship. Carter's Montreal teammate, Tim Raines, also put up big numbers throughout the 1980s, leading the league in stolen bases four years in a row, winning a batting title in 1986, and earning All-Star honors each season between 1981 and 1987. In the mid-1980s there was no better offensive player in the league than the Expo leftfielder.

In St. Louis, outfielders Willie McGee and Vince Coleman drove pitchers crazy during the late 1980s. McGee first grabbed headlines as a 23-year-old rookie during the 1982 World Series. His clutch hitting and spectacular fielding helped the Cards beat the Milwaukee Brewers in seven games. In

1985, he was joined by Coleman, whose speed and skill as a base stealer was unprecedented for a first-year player. McGee won the batting title and MVP award in 1985, while Coleman swiped 110 bases, and the Cardinals won the World Series. Two seasons later, McGee knocked in 105 runs and Coleman racked up 109 steals as St. Louis won its third pennant in six seasons. But the main cog on the Cardinals teams of the 1980s (and, for that matter, most of the 1990s) was Ozzie Smith, the best defensive shortstop ever to play the game. An acrobatic fielder who saved St. Louis countless runs with his glove, he could also be counted on for a .270 average and 30-plus stolen bases a season. The steal-happy Cards actually revolutionized pitching because they forced organizations to teach their young pitchers better moves to first and a slide step when delivering the ball to the plate. Today, it is harder to steal a base off pitchers than ever before.

When it came to combining offense and defense, the top National League players of the 1980s were Dale Murphy, Ryne Sandberg, and Mike Schmidt. In the late 1970s Murphy was touted as the catcher who would lead the Braves back to respectability. He was a failure behind the plate but blossomed when Atlanta switched him to, of all places, centerfield. The 6'5" Murphy not only learned to play the position, he won five Gold Gloves out there for his defensive excellence. The free-swinging Murphy terrorized NL pitchers throughout the decade, topping 30 homers six times and 100 RBIs five times. In 1982, he led Atlanta to the playoffs for the first time in 13 years and won the MVP. In 1983, he knocked in a career-high 121 RBIs and won the MVP again. Sandberg, the second baseman for

Ozzie Smith checks out the competition. His acrobatic skills at shortstop thrilled fans in the 1970s, 1980s, and 1990s.

Mike Schmidt drives the ball to the opposite field. Many experts consider him the best all-around third baseman ever.

the Chicago Cubs, won the MVP in 1984 when he led the long-suffering franchise to the post-season for the first time since World War II. In 1989, "Ryno" led the team to another division title. A ten-time All-Star and nine-time Gold Glover, Sandberg blended near-flawless fielding with a powerful bat—a rare combination for a second baseman. Schmidt, a huge star in the 1970s, reached his peak in the early 1980s, leading the Phillies to pennants in 1980 and 1983. He won the league home-run crown five times between 1980 and 1986 and retired in 1989 with 10 Gold Gloves.

The best pure hitter in the National League? That was Tony Gwynn, who led the league in hitting four times between 1984 and 1989. Not since Stan Musial had a player held such a death grip on the NL batting title. The San Diego Padres rightfielder led the club to the pennant in 1984 and made the All-Star team every year but one after becoming a regular. Despite using a short bat, Gwynn covered the plate as well as any left-handed hitter in history. He almost always hit the ball hard and often went an entire week between strikeouts. After toiling on mediocre teams and battling knee problems in the early 1990s, Gwynn bounced back to win several more batting titles and provided the veteran leadership the Padres needed to become pennant contenders once again.

Although no single pitcher stayed on top of his game for more than a few years in a row, NL pitching during the 1980s did feature some great single-season performances. In 1981, Fernando-mania gripped baseball, as Fernando Valenzuela of the Dodgers had one of the best rookie seasons on record. A native of Mexico, he claimed to be 20 but he looked and pitched like a player with a good 10 seasons under his belt. Despite losing a third of the 1981 season to the strike, Valenzuela won 13 games and led the league with 180 strikeouts and eight shutouts. The pudgy left-hander dazzled hitters by mixing a 90 mph fastball with a screwball comparable to Carl Hubbell's. Valenzuela packed stadiums wherever he pitched and attracted an unprecedented number of Mexican-American fans to the game. He pitched the Dodgers into the post-season three times between 1981 and 1985 and remained an effective major-league hurler into the late 1990s.

A big factor in the Dodgers 1985 division title was the mound work of Orel

Hershiser, who went 19–3 with a 2.03 ERA and led the league with an .864 winning percentage. He took full advantage of spacious Dodger Stadium that year, winning all 11 of his decisions there and allowing just one earned run a game. A tough right-hander with a riding fastball and a dipping slider, Hershiser refused to give in to hitters and usually made a big pitch when he had to. In 1988, he closed out a magnificent campaign with 59 consecutive scoreless innings, breaking former Dodger Don Drysdale's all-time mark. Hershiser shut out the Mets in the deciding game of the playoffs that year, then stymied the Oakland A's in the fall classic to bring Los Angeles its second world championship of the decade. In the process, he won the Cy Young Award and became the first player ever to win MVP honors in both the League Championship Series and the World Series during the same post-season.

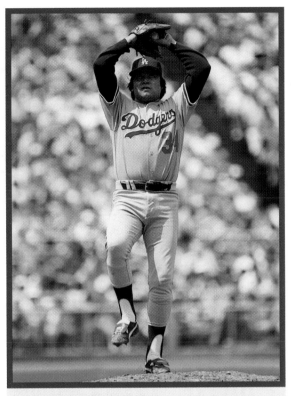

Fernando Valenzuela goes into his windup, starting with his trademark upward glance.

The National League's other great pitching story of the 1980s also turned out to be its saddest. Dwight Gooden jumped from Class-A Lynchburg right into the New York Mets starting rotation in 1984 at the age of 19 and proceeded to set baseball on its ear with a 17–9 record and 276 strikeouts in just 218 innings. That summer Gooden became the youngest player ever selected to participate in the All-Star Game, and that fall he struck out a record 43 batters over three games. The fans at Shea Stadium called him Dr. K (K being the scoring symbol for a strikeout), and posted large hand-drawn "K" signs each time he blew a hitter away. In 1985, Gooden went 24–4 with a 1.53 ERA—one of the finest seasons a pitcher ever had— and brought the Mets agonizingly close to the division title. New York won it all in

1986, and although Gooden was a major contributor to the team's world championship, he was not as effective as he had been during his first two seasons. Initially, it was thought that too many innings had been heaped upon his young arm. But eventually the truth came out: he had developed an alcohol problem. He tried and failed on several occasions to clean himself up, and though he managed to pitch well most of the time, his life continued to spin out of control until, finally, he was suspended for an entire season. Once a seeming shoo-in for the Hall of Fame, Gooden stands as one of the great wastes of natural ability in the history of sports.

The 1980s ended on a particularly sour

Pete Rose takes a cut during a 1985 contest. Baseball's all-time hit leader was banned from the game in 1989 for gambling.

note, when Pete Rose was suspended for life by baseball commissioner Bart Giamatti. The charge was gambling, and although Rose never admitted guilt, the evidence gathered by Giamatti's investigators alleged that the Cincinnati Reds manager had bet heavily on a variety of sports, including baseball games involving his own team. At the time, Rose was the most visible and popular figure in baseball and a certain first-ballot Hall of Famer. His 4,192nd hit in September 1985 had broken Ty Cobb's all-time record and diverted a lot of attention away from some of the bad things happening to baseball that year.

The Rose and Gooden stories were typical of the problems that seemed to beset baseball during the 1980s. If anyone ever questioned whether the game is a mirror of society, there was no question anymore. Baseball shared America's ills during the decade, which may explain why—despite one awful story after another—Americans continued to attend games in record num-

bers. Yet between greed, stupidity, drugs, and gambling, baseball had totally blown its chance to solidify its position as America's favorite sport. In a decade of startling prosperity, baseball had taken aim at the largest, richest, and most enthusiastic fan base in the world and shot itself in the foot.

The 1990s

When sports historians put some distance between themselves and the 1990s, chances are they will size it up as a time when a lot of long-simmering issues in baseball came boiling to the top. A lot of good things happened, and some remarkably bad things happened, and no one was ever sure what was going to happen from one week to the next. The topsy-turvy tone for the decade was set in 1991, when the World Series featured two teams that had finished dead last the season before: the Minnesota Twins and the Atlanta Braves.

Atlanta engineered its stunning turn-

The 1995 Atlanta Braves won their third pennant in five seasons. The team dominated the NL during the 1990s but did not win a World Series until 1995.

around with a formula that would serve the team well throughout the 1990s: tough pitching, a key free agent pickup, an emerging young star or two, and a smart preseason deal. Perennial losers since their glory days in the early 1980s, the Braves had been stocking themselves with high draft picks and trading for promising young pitchers for a long time. In 1991, Tom Glavine, John Smoltz, and Steve Avery—all between the ages of 21 and 25—combined with veteran Charlie Liebrandt to win 67 games. Third baseman Terry Pendleton, a key contributor to two St. Louis pennants in the 1980s, was signed by the Braves to solidify their infield, and he responded by winning the batting title and MVP. Young power hitters Ron Gant and Dave Justice combined for 53 homers, and centerfielder Otis Nixon batted .297 and swiped 72 bases upon joining the team in an unheralded April 1 trade. Smoltz beat the Astros on the final day of the season, and the Giants dropped the Dodgers to give Atlanta the division title. Avery and

Smoltz pitched the Braves past the Pirates in the NLCS and nearly dropped the Twins in the World Series, which they lost in seven thrilling games.

The Braves went on to establish the first true baseball dynasty since the Reds and Yankees in the 1970s—and the only one of the 1990s. They bolstered their offense with smart pickups, such as slugging first baseman Fred McGriff and two-sport star Deion Sanders, as well as developing young sluggers Ryan Klesko, Javier Lopez, and Chipper Jones in their well-stocked farm system. Centerfield posed a problem after Nixon tested the free agent waters prior to the 1994 season, but owner Ted Turner made sure he always had a Grade A player out there, from Roberto Kelly to Marquis Grissom to Kenny Lofton. When the Braves needed starters, they went out and got them—Greg Maddux in 1993, Denny Neagle in 1996—and pitching coach Leo Mazzone coaxed remarkable performances out of undistinguished relievers like Kent

Mercker, Mike Stanton, Juan Berenguer, Greg McMichael, and Alejandro Pena. In 1995, Mark Wohlers finally harnessed his 100 mph heater and became a dominant closer. One way or another, Atlanta was able to put an awesome team on the field each season, winning the National League pennant in 1991 and 1992, and again in 1995 and 1996.

The Twins built no such dynasty after their World Series triumph in 1991. They had risen from worst to first in the American League West on the young arms of second-year starters Scott Erickson and Kevin Tapani, with an assist from free-agent signee Jack Morris. The Twins won despite the fact that not a single one of their position players had a career year. Balance was the key, as the team had a productive all-around performer at each position, including Kirby Puckett in centerfield, Kent Hrbek at first base, and Rookie of the Year Chuck Knoblauch at second base. In 1992, the Twins finished second and then spent the next five seasons struggling to reach the .500 mark.

The big blow was the loss of Morris, who left the team after his magnificent performance in the 1991 World Series and signed with the Toronto Blue Jays. "Jack the Cat" understood how 1990s-style free agency worked before a lot of general managers did. As a star pitcher, he was a paid mercenary and as such was nothing more than part of a math equation. If a team was getting 5 to 10 wins out of its worst starter, it could simply sign Morris, who was good for 15 to 20. With everything else being equal, that team could expect to experience a 10-game rise in the standings. That was worth a lot of money, especially to a team that had just finished a half-dozen games out of first.

The veteran starter won 21 games for the Blue Jays in 1992 and led them to the World Series, where they beat the Braves. Morris would move to the Indians in 1994, and he helped pitch that team into pennant contention for the first time since 1959. Morris was the first of many pitchers who peddled their services to the highest bidder during the 1990s. Teams, in fact, became a bit obsessed with signing pitchers. Every winter, at least five teams would invest millions on a top hurler in the belief that he would bring them the pennant the following fall. The problem was, if the rest of the team did not do its job, those millions were wasted. As salaries for superstars quadrupled between 1990 and 1995, the risk factors involved in signing a big-name free agent had to be addressed. So teams devised a way of cutting their losses if things did not work out.

New Free Agency

David Cone, one of the most consistent and coveted right-handed starters in baseball during the 1990s, is an example of how free agency was changing. In 1992, the Mets signed Bobby Bonilla and Bret Saberhagen to huge contracts. Bonilla played poorly, Saberhagen got hurt, and the Mets tumbled to the bottom of their division. Cone, meanwhile, was pitching beautifully. Having already committed tens of millions to a group of core players, New York knew it would not have the money to sign Cone after the season, when he was due to become a free agent. Rather than getting nothing for Cone, New York traded him to the Blue Jays in August for a pair of prospects. Cone did his job for the Jays, helping them win the World Series. After the season, he declared himself a

Three Strikes ... They're Out!

One of those owners was Bud Selig of the Milwaukee Brewers, who assumed the post of baseball's acting commissioner after the owners decided to get rid of commissioner Fay Vincent in 1992 and revamp the office they had created back in 1920. The players were getting too much power, and the owners believed that Vincent would side with them during the next round of bargaining sessions. With Selig looking out for their interests, the small-market teams could be sure that they would not be sold out by rich clubs who could afford gigantic payrolls, such as the Yankees and Dodgers.

What the teams in the small markets proposed was a restructuring of revenues. They wanted a share of the millions big-market clubs were making from local and cable television, and they also proposed that team payrolls be limited so that the rich franchises would be prevented from pushing salaries up through the roof. Only then could such teams as the Padres, Pirates, and Mariners be assured of putting a competitive team on the field. After much complaining, the big-market owners agreed to the plan. And all of the owners agreed that changes needed to be made in the salary arbitration process, which they felt was weighted very heavily in favor of the players.

When the owners presented these ideas to the players, they refused to listen. They were unwilling to give up any of the gains they had made since the advent of free agency and refuted the claim by owners that only nine teams were turning a profit. On August 11, the players walked off the job. They believed the owners would give up

Acting commissioner Bud Selig answers reporters' questions. Many observers felt that the lack of a full-time commissioner hurt baseball during the 1990s.

their demands before the season ended, for a cancellation of the playoffs and World Series—big moneymakers for baseball—would prove a financial disaster. But the owners held their ground, and for the first time since 1904, there was no post-season play.

The abrupt end to the 1994 baseball season was a public-relations disaster for baseball and particularly heartbreaking for baseball fans. During the first 117 games, several of the sport's top stars were on pace to threaten the all-time home-run mark. Ken Griffey, Jr., a marvelous young player for the Seattle Mariners, cranked out an AL-high 40 home runs. Right behind him was Frank Thomas of the Chicago White Sox with 38. Either could have eclipsed Roger

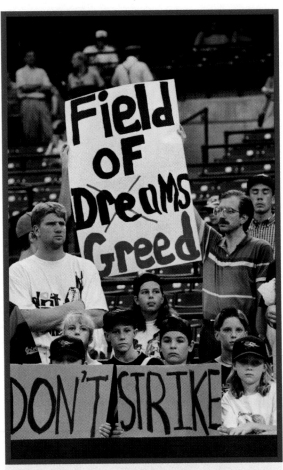

On August 11, 1994, Orioles fans let the players know what they think of the threatened strike. The players walked out the next day, and the following month team owners canceled the season and all post-season play.

when the season stopped. Would he have been the first man in half a century to bat .400? The world would never know.

Pumping Up the Numbers

The 1994 slugging binge actually began a year earlier, when a pair of expansion teams, the Colorado Rockies and Florida Marlins, joined the National League. During the early 1990s, pitching had become very thin, and many teams struggled to find 10 decent hurlers to form a staff. With two new baseball teams in action, there simply was not enough quality pitching to go around. In game after game, pitchers who were not ready to face big-time hitters were being thrust into crucial situations, and the hitters went to town. From 1992 to 1993, slugging averages in the NL jumped 31 points, and from 1993 to 1994 they jumped another 16. In the AL, slugging rose 23 points from 1992 to 1993 and 26 more points in 1994.

Bad pitching alone, however, could not account for what happened. A lot of the jump in offense had to do with the fact that hitters were beefing up and pumping iron—a trend that had been developing for years. Throughout baseball history, the common wisdom had been that if hitters wanted to get stronger, they should do so by hitting more. Lifting weights was seen as being detrimental, for it added too much bulky muscle mass to areas that had to be quick and flexible. But with advances in weight training and nutritional aids, the ballplayers of the late 1980s and early 1990s—most notably Mark McGwire, Ken Caminiti, and Brady Anderson—were able to develop massive forearms, biceps, shoulders, and

Maris's record 61 home runs in the 45 games that were never played. In the National League, Barry Bonds socked 37 home runs for the Giants, while teammate Matt Williams led the majors with 43 round-trippers. In Houston, first baseman Jeff Bagwell hit 39 homers and slugged .750, which was the second-highest mark in National League history. Tony Gwynn, meanwhile, had his average up to .394

chest muscles without negatively affecting their swings. This showed up in the form of extra-base hits and home runs; fly balls and line drives that had once been catchable were flying a few feet further, hitting the fences or carrying over them. And in the delicate balance between offense and defense, this was enough to topple the scales. With the Arizona Diamondbacks and Tampa Bay Devil Rays beginning play in 1998, baseball people are predicting that many single-season offensive records will fall by the turn of the century.

Hitting Stars of the 1990s

With the overall lack of consistent, quality pitching in the majors during the 1990s, one might be tempted to discount the achievements of baseball's top hitters. That would be a mistake. Even the old-timers have to admit that the hitting stars of the 1990s are bigger, stronger, and faster than they were. They also have to deal with better late-inning closers and a wider variety of pitches, including the dreaded split-fingered fastball. A .320 hitter in the 1990s is every bit as good as a .320 hitter in the 1970s, 1960s, or 1950s, and probably a lot better than a .320 hitter in the 1920s and 1930s. Who were the top offensive players of the 1990s?

The American League has featured a quintet of classic sluggers in Mark McGwire, Frank Thomas, Cecil Fielder, Albert Belle, and Juan Gonzalez. McGwire (who finished the 1997 season with the NL St. Louis Cardinals) was averaging 8.37 home runs per 100 at bats, placing him second all-time to Babe Ruth, who averaged 8.50 per 100 at bats. Had McGwire not lost the 1993 and 1994 seasons to injury, he might have

been closing in on 500 homers by his 34th birthday. Thomas was already halfway to 500 when he was 29. At 6'5" and 240 lbs., the Chicago White Sox first baseman ranks among the biggest, strongest .300 hitters who have ever played—he is certainly one of the most feared. Thomas brings something else to his craft—patience. He will not offer at a pitch if he feels he cannot drive it, which means pitchers must either give him something he can hit or walk him. In his first five full seasons, "The Big Hurt" led the AL in bases on balls four times. Fielder, whose progress was stalled in the Toronto system during the 1980s, took a huge gamble and left the majors to play in Japan. There he proved he could be a big-time hitter, and in 1990 the Detroit Tigers took a chance and brought him back to American baseball. Their gamble paid off handsomely as "Big Daddy" blasted 51 homers and led the AL in RBIs and slugging. Fielder hit a total of 245 home runs in six-plus seasons for the Tigers. With two months to go in the 1996 season, he was traded to the New York Yankees and played a key role in the team's remarkable world championship run. Belle was the key to the resurgence of the Cleveland Indians, who won the AL pennant in 1995. He won Cleveland's leftfield job in 1991 and averaged 38 home runs a year and led the league in RBIs three times during his six full seasons with the team. In 1995, he collected 50 doubles and 50 homers in the same season, which ranks among the greatest batting feats of all time. Gonzalez, an outfielder for the Texas Rangers, also won a starting job in 1991. In 1992 and 1993, he led the AL in home runs, establishing himself as the finest power hitter ever to come out of Puerto Rico. In 1996, Gonzalez picked up the Rangers and carried them on his back all summer long. His 47 home runs and 144 RBIs brought the franchise its first division title since moving to Texas in 1972 and earned him the Most Valuable Player Award. In the playoffs, he clubbed five home runs in four games and nearly toppled the Yankees single-handedly.

The best all-around player in the AL during the 1990s has been Ken Griffey, Jr. Even when he broke in with the Mariners in 1989 at the age of 19, Griffey could do just about everything well. A consistent .300 hitter who developed awesome power by the age of 23, Griffey set the league on fire with 56 home runs in 1997. And when he gets hot, there is no stopping him. In the field, he is just as good, and it may be a

Juan Gonzalez waits for a pitch. The Rangers slugger led the AL in home runs in 1992 and 1993.

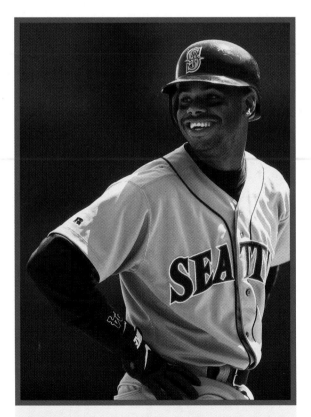

Ken Griffey Jr. smiles after getting a hit.

very long time before another centerfielder beats him out for the Gold Glove. The best all-around player in the NL during the 1990s has been Barry Bonds. The Griffey-Bonds debate has been raging for years and will probably keep fans busy through the end of the century. So far, Bonds gets the edge. He has tremendous power and enviable patience at the plate; defensively, he is right up there with the best leftfielders in history. Bonds, whose father Bobby was an All-Star during the 1970s, did something his dad never did when he won the MVP with the Pittsburgh Pirates in 1990. He won the award again in 1992, then signed a record-breaking free-agent deal with the San Francisco Giants. The team was rewarded the very next season, when Bonds led the NL in home runs, RBIs, on-base percentage, and slugging and won the MVP for a third time. A leadoff hitter at the start of his career, he has continued to steal bases even after moving down into the middle of the order and will probably retire as the first player with 400 homers and 400 steals.

Other noteworthy National Leaguers during the 1990s have been Matt Williams, Mike Piazza, Jeff Bagwell, and Barry Larkin. For a while, Williams—a brilliant fielder with a deadly home-run swing— looked as if he might give Mike Schmidt a run for his money as history's top third baseman. At 24, he was the top RBI man in the league, but injuries and inconsistency plagued him throughout the first seven years of his career. Still, when Williams is healthy and in the groove, there is no one better in baseball. Piazza, a high-school third baseman who learned to catch so he could make it to the majors faster, established himself as the best offensive back-

stop since Johnny Bench after breaking in with the Dodgers at the tail end of 1992. In his first five full seasons, the Los Angeles star averaged .335 with 33 home runs and 100 RBIs, and his .638 slugging average in 1997 is 51 points higher than the best mark

Three-time NL MVP Barry Bonds watches his blast head for the seats.

Greg Maddux gets ready to release a circle change-up. The righthander was the most effective NL pitcher in the 1990s.

numbers despite playing in the toughest hitter's ballpark in all of baseball. Larkin won the MVP in 1995, when he hit .319, stole 51 bases, and earned his second straight Gold Glove as the NL's top defensive shortstop. In 1996, he played even better, leading the Reds in runs, doubles, RBIs, homers, walks, slugging, and stolen bases. A consistent .300 hitter since 1988 and a spectacular fielder from his first day in the majors, Larkin has put up impressive numbers despite being plagued by an endless string of injuries.

Pitching Stars of the 1990s

Despite baseball's power surge during the 1990s, there have been a few pitchers who found a way to thrive. In the American League, Mike Mussina, Andy Pettitte, Kevin Appier, Randy Johnson, and Roger Clemens have been consistent winners. In the National League, Tom Glavine and John Smoltz of the Braves have won Cy Young awards, and Kevin Brown—a former 21-game winner in the American League—transformed the expansion Marlins into pennant contenders. But the best of them all has been Greg Maddux. Not since Lefty Grove shut down the sluggers of the 1920s and 1930s has a hurler so dramatically set himself apart from his peers. Maddux might just be the smartest pitcher ever to play the game. He has exhibited an uncanny ability to make good hitters take bad swings at his best pitches, which is really the whole idea of pitching.

To be a consistent winner in the big leagues, a pitcher must be able to throw three different pitches for strikes. Maddux throws four different pitches (including a

ever turned in by Bench. Bagwell, who was stuck behind Wade Boggs in Boston, was traded to the Houston Astros organization in 1990 and switched to first base. He responded by winning Rookie of the Year honors in 1991, and three years later he won the MVP when he turned in one of the best offensive seasons in history. An aggressive and fearless hitter, Bagwell has put up great

90 mph fastball) and can hit either the inside or outside corner with each. He spent the first part of his career pitching for the Cubs in homer-happy Wrigley Field. In his final season there he posted a 2.18 ERA, which was 1.32 points below the league average. In 1993, Maddux signed as a free agent with the Braves and turned in a 2.36 ERA, which was 1.68 points below the league average. In his next two seasons, while hitters were feasting on NL pitching, Maddux recorded ERAs of 1.56 and 1.63. In those seasons, the NL ERA hovered well over four runs per game. When fans look back at the 1990s a few years from now, they will not only regard Maddux as the decade's best pitcher, but maybe even its most influential player.

The high-school pitchers of the 1980s who emulated Nolan Ryan and Roger Clemens are now serving up 3-1 fastballs to the likes of Larry Walker and Alex Rodriguez, who in turn are depositing them in the far reaches of the bleachers. Are today's teenage pitchers emulating Greg Maddux? If so, perhaps young hurlers in the coming century will understand how to disarm free-swinging sluggers with a repertoire of deceptively tempting deliveries. Perhaps in Maddux's success lie clues to the next trend in baseball. It is not nearly as far-fetched an idea as it might seem. The hitters may continue battering the pitchers for a few more years, but if baseball teaches us one thing it is that when the pendulum swings too far in one direction, it always finds a way to swing back.

The Future

Where is baseball headed beyond the year 2000? No one can say for sure. What is cer-

A group of young Mets fans enjoys a beautiful day at Shea Stadium. Although baseball is going through a difficult period, the national pastime still draws millions.

tain, however, is that as the game prepares to compete for America's entertainment dollar, it is armed with two important weapons—a century-and-a-half of tradition and an ability to change with the times. For every innovation that comes along there will be something else that reminds fans of baseball's connection to the past. And that balance should also translate right on down to the playing field, where the give-and-take between pitchers and hitters will continue to evolve, yet never go so far in either direction as to undermine the integrity of the game. Most important of all for baseball's future is that it should continue to mirror society in the United States and—as it grows to embrace a more global audience—one day reflect the hopes, dreams, and desires of people the world over.

A Baseball Timeline

1834 Rules for the child's game of base ball are printed in a popular book on sports; batters are instructed to run clockwise after hitting the ball.

1845 The Knickerbocker Base Ball Club is formed.

1846 The first recorded baseball game between two clubs takes place in Hoboken, N.J.

1849 The Knickerbockers adopt baseball's first uniforms: blue pants, white shirts, and straw hats.

1853 Newspaper coverage of baseball games begins.

1855 The New York metropolitan area boasts more than a dozen clubs, making it the center of the baseball world.

1858 The National Association of Base Ball Players is formed, marking the beginning of organized baseball; admission is charged to games for the first time.

1859 The first college baseball game is played between Williams and Amherst in Massachusetts.

1860 The Gotham Club of New York makes baseball's first "road trip," traveling north from Manhattan to play clubs in Albany, Troy, and Buffalo.

1865 Interest in baseball intensifies after the Civil War, with clubs springing up all over the country.

1866 The National Association of Base Ball Players counts among its members more than 200 clubs; a migration of top players from east to west begins when teams from Pittsburgh to Chicago begin offering high salaries.

1869 The Cincinnati Red Stockings go 56–0 on a national tour.

1871 The National Association of Professional Baseball Players, baseball's first professional league, is formed; the Great Chicago Fire forces the White Stockings to play their final games on the road, and they lose the pennant; the first recorded game between a team of white players and a team of black players takes place in Chicago.

1872 The Boston Red Stockings win their first of four consecutive National Association pennants.

1874 The Boston and Philadelphia clubs travel to England in an attempt to popularize baseball overseas.

1875 Joe Borden of the Athletics pitches baseball's first no-hitter; the first catcher's mask is used during a college game; the first women's professional game is played.

1876 Eight members of the National Association agree to form the National League; the Chicago White Stockings win the first NL pennant; several players, including Al Spalding of the Chicago White Stockings, begin using thinly padded gloves in the field.

1878 Paul Hines of the Providence Grays leads the National League with four home runs, 50 RBIs, and a .358 average to become history's first Triple Crown winner.

1879 Player contracts include the reserve clause for the first time; the Providence Grays erect a screen behind home plate to protect fans from foul balls—that section of the grandstand had formerly been nicknamed the "slaughter pen."

1880 Two amateur teams meet on Nantasket Beach in Massachusetts in the first baseball game played under artificial lighting.

1881 The pitcher's box is moved to 50 feet, 5 feet further away from home plate; Oberlin College's Moses Fleetwood Walker becomes the first black man to play for a college team; Roger Connor of the Troy Trojans hits the first grand slam. He would retire with 136 home runs, a mark that holds up until Babe Ruth comes along.

1882 The American Association begins play; NL and AA champions meet in an impromptu "World Series"; Paul Hines begins using sunglasses in the outfield; the Worcester Ruby Legs and Providence Grays split the first doubleheader in major-league history.

1883 Browns owner Chris Von Der Ahe describes St. Louis rooters as "fanatics," leading to the term "fan."

1884 The Union Association is formed, marking the first time three major leagues are in operation simultaneously; pitchers are allowed to deliver the ball from above the waist for the first time.

1885 Major-league catchers begin wearing chest protectors, although they have been available for nearly 10 years.

1886 Guy Hecker of the Louisville Colonels hits three home runs in a game and wins the AA batting title two years after leading the league in pitching victories; the first sets of baseball cards are produced by Goodwin & Co., Lone Jack Cigarette Co., and Lorillard Tobacco Co.; given away in packs of cigarettes, these cards today sell for between $500 and $10,000 each.

1887 Chicago White Stockings superstar King Kelly is sold for a record $10,000 to the Boston Beaneaters; Cap Anson takes the White Stockings to Arkansas for baseball's first "spring training"; the first major set of baseball cards is issued by Goodwin & Co. and distributed in packs of Old Judge cigarettes; the set features more than 500 players from more than three dozen major- and minor-league teams; Tip O'Neill of the St. Louis Browns wins the American Association Triple Crown; Cap Anson refuses to play an exhibition game pitched by George Stovey, a black star of the International League, which leads to a six-decade ban of blacks by organized baseball.

1888 Tim Keefe of the New York Giants wins a record 19 straight games; Ernest Thayer publishes the famous poem "Casey at the Bat."

1889 Baseball settles on the modern balls and strikes ratio: four balls for a walk, three strikes for an out—although foul balls are not counted as strikes; the NL pennant goes down to the final day of the season for the first time in history.

1890 The Players League begins play, but fails after just one season; specially designed catcher's mitts come into use.

1891 Teams are allowed to substitute players for any reason, not just for injuries.

1892 Restrictions on trading players are eased, and manager Ned Hanlon of the Baltimore Orioles is the first to use this method to restructure a team; Benjamin Harrison becomes the first U.S. president to attend a baseball game.

1893 The distance between the pitching rubber and home plate is established at the modern 60' 6"; pitching mounds are optional; the NL and AA merge to form the League-Association, but it is commonly called the National League.

1894 Hugh Duffy of the Boston Beaneaters wins the Triple Crown with 18 home runs, 145 RBIs, and an awesome .440 average. His teammate, Bobby Lowe, becomes the first player to hit four home runs in a game; the Temple Cup—a post-season competition between the NL's top two teams—proves a poor substitute for the World Series.

1895 Strikes are called on foul tips but not on regular foul balls, and it is up to the umpires to distinguish between the two.

1896 Baseball cards all but disappear when the country's major tobacco companies form a monopoly and no longer need to compete with one another.

1897 Cap Anson becomes the first player to amass 3,000 career hits; Willie Keeler of the Baltimore Orioles hits safely in an NL-record 44 straight games.

1900 The NL drops its Baltimore, Cleveland, Louisville, and Washington clubs, consolidating to eight teams; the modern home plate is unveiled for the start of the season; the Western League changes its name to the American

League and begins play in eight cities, including Chicago.

1901 The AL moves into Boston and Philadelphia and begins offering NL players huge pay increases to jump leagues; Napoleon Lajoie, the top player to join the AL, wins the Triple Crown with 14 home runs, 125 RBIs, and a .426 average.

1902 Ed Delehanty of Washington becomes the first player to win a batting crown in more than one league. He led the NL in hitting with the Phillies in 1899; the AL out-draws the NL by more than half a million fans, prompting a "peace agreement."

1903 Both leagues begin counting foul balls as strikes; the first World Series is played, with the NL Pittsburgh Pirates falling to the AL Boston Pilgrims, five games to three; the first movies of baseball players appear, featuring Lajoie and Cleveland teammate Harry Bay in action during a post-season series against the Reds.

1904 Jack Chesbro sets a modern record by winning 41 games for the New York Highlanders but blows their pennant chances with a wild pitch in the season's final game; manager John McGraw of the pennant-winning New York Giants refuses to play the AL-champion Boston Pilgrims because of a personal feud with AL president Ban Johnson; the World Series is

made an official part of baseball thereafter.

1905 Giants star Roger Bresnahan designs an air-cushioned batting helmet and special shin guards for catchers; Vic Willis proves it takes a good pitcher to lose 20 games when he drops a record 29 decisions but gains entry into the Hall of Fame 90 years later; pitching reaches its pinnacle as every game of the World Series between the New York Giants and the Philadelphia Athletics is a shutout.

1908 The first electronic scoreboard is unveiled; Christy Mathewson of the New York Giants establishes the modern NL mark for wins with 37.

1909 The importation of Turkish tobacco creates opportunities for new companies to compete in the U.S. market, and the result is an explosion of baseball cards, which are used as incentives for fans to stay loyal to a particular brand; between 1909 and 1911, more than 2,000 different cards are available nationally; Ty Cobb wins the AL Triple Crown.

1910 President William Taft starts an American tradition when he throws out the first ball on Opening Day; Cy Young wins his 500th game.

1911 A new rule requires teams to wear light and dark versions of their uniform during home games and road games, respectively; a new ball with a rubber-and-cork center is adopted by the major leagues and offense soars; Ty Cobb wins the first Chalmers Award, a forerunner of the Most Valuable Player Award.

1912 Heinie Zimmerman, the forgotten fourth player in the Chicago Cubs famous Tinker-to-Evers-to-Chance infield, wins the NL Triple Crown; Rube Marquard of the New York Giants wins 19 games in a row.

1914 The Federal League declares itself a third major league and begins signing AL and NL players, including stars Joe Tinker and George Stovall.

1915 The Federal League sues Organized Baseball, claiming it is a monopoly. The suit is settled out of court and Federal League owners are paid a huge sum to fold their circuit at year's end; the New York Yankees begin wearing pinstriped uniforms; Ty Cobb wins his fifth batting title in a row.

1916 The Chicago Cubs decide to let fans keep balls hit into the stands; it would be another 25 years before all clubs adhere to this policy; the Cleveland Indians become the first team to wear uniform numbers, although the experiment is quickly abandoned.

1917 Grover Cleveland Alexander leads the NL in wins for the fourth year in a row; America's entry into World War I wreaks havoc on baseball: dozens of major leaguers join the military, and enlistment among minor leaguers causes eight of 20 professional leagues to fold prior to the 1918 season; to demonstrate baseball's patriotism, the "Star Spangled Banner" is played before many major-league games, and players perform close-order marching drills with bats on their shoulders instead of rifles.

1919 Eight players on the Chicago White Sox conspire to lose the World Series to the underdog Cincinnati Reds.

1920 The spitball and other doctored pitches are outlawed; Cleveland Indians shortstop Ray Chapman dies after being hit in the head by a pitch; a new fielder's glove with a pocket and webbing is introduced; Babe Ruth is purchased from the Boston Red Sox by the New York Yankees for a record sum of $100,000 and proceeds to demolish his own home-run record with 54 round-trippers; George Sisler of the St. Louis Browns collects a record 257 base hits; Rube Foster organizes the country's top black barnstorming clubs into the Negro National League, which operates on and off in several midwestern cities until 1947.

1921 Because of the Chapman tragedy, umpires are instructed to keep a clean ball in the game at all times. Batting and slugging averages soar as a result; the first broadcast of a major-league game is aired on KDKA radio in Pittsburgh, and action from the World Series is reported live by WJZ in Newark, New Jersey; Babe Ruth finishes the season with a record 59 homers and becomes baseball's all-time champ when he hits his 137th career home run.

1922 Rogers Hornsby of the St. Louis Cardinals wins the NL Triple Crown, but crosstown rival George Sisler of the Browns receives the new League Award as most valuable player.

1923 Ty Cobb eclipses Honus Wagner's career record for hits; Babe Ruth draws a record 170 walks; the Eastern Colored League is established in such major cities as New York and Baltimore.

1924 The New York Giants win their fourth consecutive NL pennant; Rogers Hornsby sets a modern record with a .424 batting average.

1925 Rogers Hornsby becomes the first player to win a second Triple Crown, taking his fifth straight batting title in the process.

1927 Babe Ruth establishes a new record with 60 home runs; Ty Cobb gets his 4,000th hit.

1929 The first public address system is installed in the Polo Grounds, replacing the traditional cardboard megaphone; Grover Cleveland Alexander retires, believing he has

broken Christy Mathewson's NL record for wins with 373. Years later, a review of the records shows that Mathewson also had 373.

1930 The AL makes uniform numbers mandatory for all teams; Hack Wilson of the Chicago Cubs sets an NL record with 56 home runs and a major-league mark with 190 RBIs.

1931 The baseball writers begin voting for league MVPs, establishing an award that continues to this day. Lefty Grove and Frankie Frisch are the first winners; 17-year-old Jackie Mitchell becomes the first woman to pitch for a minor-league team, appearing for the Memphis Lookouts in an exhibition game against the New York Yankees.

1932 Babe Ruth appears to call his shot before slugging a dramatic homer against the Cubs in the World Series; former Indians star Jack Graney moves up to the radio booth, the first ex–major leaguer to make this transition.

1933 The first All-Star Game is played in Chicago, with the AL winning 4-2; Philadelphia has a Triple Crown season, as Jimmie Foxx of the Athletics and Chuck Klein of the Phillies lead their respective leagues in home runs, RBIs, and batting average.

1934 Pittsburgh becomes the last major-league city to lift its law against Sunday baseball; the Cincinnati

Reds become the first team to travel by airplane; Lou Gehrig wins the AL Triple Crown.

1935 The Cincinnati Reds host the Philadelphia Phillies in the first major-league night game. Minor league and amateur teams had been playing under the lights regularly for more than a decade.

1936 The Hall of Fame is established, and its first five members—Ty Cobb, Honus Wagner, Babe Ruth, Christy Mathewson, and Walter Johnson—are inducted.

1937 Joe Medwick of the St. Louis Cardinals becomes the last National Leaguer to win the Triple Crown; the Negro American League is formed, operating in the South and Midwest.

1938 Johnny Vander Meer of the Cincinnati Reds pitches back-to-back no-hitters against the Braves and Dodgers.

1939 A college game between Princeton and Columbia becomes the first televised contest in baseball history; Lou Gehrig becomes the first player to have his uniform number retired; the New York Yankees win their fourth consecutive AL pennant; Little League Baseball plays its first official season.

1941 Joe DiMaggio hits safely in 56 consecutive games, and Ted Williams becomes the last player to bat .400; several members of the Brooklyn Dodgers begin wearing batting helmets; the U.S. military begins the draft in anticipation of war with Japan and Germany, and Hank Greenberg is the first big star tabbed for service.

1942 Ted Williams wins the AL Triple Crown.

1943 A newly constructed wartime baseball proves so hard to hit that old balls from the previous season are dusted off and rushed into play.

1944 With major-league talent drastically depleted by the war, the hapless St. Louis Browns capture the pennant with only their second winning season in 15 years.

1945 Wartime shortages force teams to use a 15-year-old pitcher and a one-armed outfielder; the Washington Senators nearly become the first team to go from worst to first but lose the AL pennant on the season's final day when outfielder Bingo Binks loses a flyball in the sun during extra innings; the Brooklyn Dodgers sign Jackie Robinson to a minor-league contract.

1946 Entrepreneur Bill Veeck heads a group of investors that purchases the Indians, and within two years his zany ballpark promotions and eye for talent combine to draw a record 2.6 million fans to Municipal Stadium and produce the first Cleveland pennant in almost 30 years; the New York

Yankees become the first team to travel by air all season long.

1947 Jackie Robinson debuts for the Dodgers and is named Rookie of the Year in the first year of the award's existence; Ted Williams wins his second Triple Crown; the Little League World Series is held for the first time, in Williamsport, Pennsylvania; the World Series is televised coast-to-coast for the first time.

1949 Jackie Robinson becomes the first black batting champ and MVP.

1950 Connie Mack manages his 50th and final season with the Philadelphia Athletics; Jim Konstanty of the Philadelphia Phillies becomes the first relief pitcher to win the MVP; 37-year-old Ray Dandridge of the Minneapolis Millers becomes the first black player named MVP of a minor league.

1951 Bobby Thomson's ninth-inning playoff homer delivers the pennant to the New York Giants in the most dramatic end to a season in baseball history; a midget named Eddie Gaedel comes to bat for the St. Louis Browns in another one of owner Bill Veeck's wild promotional stunts.

1952 Topps Chewing Gum produces the first set of large-format color baseball cards, sparking an all-out war with industry rival Bowman. During the heat of this competition, kids could get as many as nine cards for a penny.

1953 Although franchise shifts had been contemplated as early as 1916, the first team to actually move is the Braves, from Boston to Milwaukee. They are called the "Miracle Braves" after vaulting all the way to second place; the Yankees win their fifth straight pennant.

1954 The St. Louis Browns move east and become the Baltimore Orioles; a new rule compels players to bring their gloves with them when their team is at bat (for decades, players had left their gloves out at their positions); with the doors of major-league baseball now open to black stars, the Negro American League plays its final season. Several teams continue as barnstorming outfits; *Sports Illustrated* begins publication.

1955 The Philadelphia Athletics move to Kansas City; Robin Roberts of the Philadelphia Phillies leads the NL in wins for the fourth consecutive season; in their sixth World Series meeting with the Yankees in 15 years, the Dodgers finally win it all in seven games.

1956 Topps absorbs rival Bowman to become the dominant producer of baseball cards in the United Sates for the next 25 years; Dale Long of the Pittsburgh Pirates slugs homers in eight consecutive games; Brooklyn's Don Newcombe wins the first Cy

Young Award; Don Larsen, who is almost cut in spring training, pitches a perfect game against the Dodgers in the World Series.

1957 Batting helmets become mandatory in the American League. Jackie Robinson refuses to be traded from the Dodgers to the Giants and chooses to retire.

1958 Major-league baseball makes its move to the West Coast as the Brooklyn Dodgers transfer to Los Angeles and the New York Giants relocate to San Francisco.

1959 Pittsburgh Pirate reliever Elroy Face goes 18–1 to set an all-time mark with a .947 winning percentage.

1960 Baseball begins keeping track of saves; player names begin appearing on uniforms for the first time.

1961 The Los Angeles Angels and a new version of the Washington Senators are added to the American League's eight teams. Roger Maris of the Yankees hits a record 61 home runs after the schedule is expanded from 154 to 162 games.

1962 The National League expands to 10 teams, adding the New York Mets and Houston Colt .45s; Jackie Robinson is the first black player inducted into the Hall of Fame; Buck O'Neill, a former star of the Negro Leagues, becomes the first black to coach in the majors with the Chicago Cubs.

1963 The strike zone is enlarged and the mound raised in order to curb the surge in power hitting caused by expansion; Mickey Mantle hits the Yankee Stadium facade with a monstrous home run, marking the fifth time he nearly hits a ball entirely out of the cavernous ballpark; 42-year-old Warren Spahn registers his 13th career 20-win season.

1964 The Yankees win five consecutive pennants for the second time, and their 14th in 16 seasons; Masanori Murakami of the Giants becomes the first Japanese player to make a major-league roster.

1965 Sandy Koufax of the Los Angeles Dodgers sets a modern record for strikeouts with 382; fearing it will lose its best players to American baseball, Japan demands the return of Masanori Murakami; the major leagues hold their first draft, allowing teams to select high-school and college players in reverse order of the previous year's finish. The first player selected is Rick Monday, who plays in the majors until 1984; the first game played on artificial turf takes place in the Houston Astrodome; Emmett Ashford becomes baseball's first black umpire.

1966 After being traded by the Reds, Frank Robinson leads the Orioles to the AL pennant and wins the Triple Crown.

1967 Carl Yastrzemski wins the Triple

Crown and leads the Red Sox to victory in the tightest pennant race in AL history.

1968 Baseball goes west again, as the Kansas City A's move to Oakland; the flaw in the rule changes made in 1963 become obvious when Bob Gibson of the Cardinals posts a 1.12 ERA yet still loses nine games, and Carl Yastrzemski of the Red Sox wins the AL batting title with a .301 mark. Denny McLain of the Tigers becomes the first 30-game winner since 1934.

1969 The major leagues expand to 24 teams with the addition of the San Diego Padres, Montreal Expos, Kansas City Royals, and Seattle Pilots. Each league is split into two divisions and a League Championship Series is created to determine pennant winners; the strike zone is reduced and pitching mounds lowered in order to restore the balance between hitters and pitchers; the New York Mets become the first expansion club to win the World Series; Curt Flood of the Cardinals, a 14-year veteran, refuses to be traded to the Phillies, calling the reserve clause a form of slavery.

1970 Flood sues Major League Baseball for violation of U.S. antitrust statutes and loses. His actions, however, set the stage for free agency; the Pilots become the Milwaukee Brewers after just one year; Willie Mays becomes the first black player to join the 3,000-hit club.

1971 The Hall of Fame opens its doors to former Negro League players, enshrining pitcher Satchel Paige; the first World Series night game is played.

1973 The AL begins using the designated hitter; Nolan Ryan of the California Angels sets a new mark record with 383 strikeouts and pitches the first of his seven career no-hitters; Roberto Clemente, who died on New Year's Eve in a plane crash, becomes the first Hispanic player inducted into the Hall of Fame.

1974 Hank Aaron hits home runs with his first two swings of the season to eclipse Babe Ruth's all-time mark of 714 home runs; Dodger reliever Mike Marshall appears in a record 106 games; Catfish Hunter becomes baseball's first free agent.

1975 Bob Watson of the Houston Astros scores the millionth run in major-league history; Frank Robinson of the Cleveland Indians becomes major-league baseball's first black manager; Sadahuru Oh wins his second straight Japanese League Triple Crown; America "rediscovers" baseball during the World Series, thanks to innovative camera work, several rainouts, and seven dramatic games between the Reds and Red Sox.

1977 The American League expands,

adding the Toronto Blue Jays and Seattle Mariners.

1978 Pete Rose of the Cincinnati Reds ties the NL record with a 44-game hitting streak; Sadahuru Oh of Japan's Yomiuri Giants eclipses Hank Aaron's professional record for home runs. He retires in 1981 with 868.

1981 A mid-season player strike forces the leagues to play a "second half" and add another tier of playoffs to determine division champions. The Cincinnati Reds fail to finish first in the NL West in either half of the season and miss the playoffs despite having the best record in the major leagues; Donruss and Fleer win the right to produce baseball cards, setting off an explosion of card sets that continues to this day.

1982 Rickey Henderson of the Oakland Athletics steals a record 130 bases.

1983 Cal Ripken, Jr, of the Baltimore Orioles becomes the first player to play in every inning of every one of his team's regular-season and post-season games.

1985 Pete Rose surpasses Ty Cobb as baseball's all-time hit leader.

1988 Don Mattingly of the New York Yankees slugs homers in eight consecutive games.

1989 Pete Rose is suspended from baseball for gambling; an earthquake causes a long postponement of the World Series between two Bay Area teams, the San Francisco Giants and the Oakland A's.

1990 Cecil Fielder, who chose to play in Japan instead of sit on the Toronto bench, returns to the majors and clubs 51 home runs for the Tigers. His success focuses much attention on Japanese baseball, setting the stage for several Japanese pitchers to come to the majors.

1991 Nolan Ryan of the Texas Rangers hurls his seventh career no-hitter; the Atlanta Braves and Minnesota Twins rise from last place the season before to win their respective league pennants. The two clubs meet in one of the most exciting World Series ever played.

1992 The owners oust commissioner Fay Vincent, eliminating the office that had served as the final word on all baseball matters since 1921; the Toronto Blue Jays become the first non-U.S. team to win the World Series.

1993 The National League expands by two teams with the addition of the Colorado Rockies and Florida Marlins; Ken Griffey, Jr., of the Seattle Mariners slugs homers in eight consecutive games.

1994 Each league is realigned into three divisions, with a "wild card" team gaining a post-season berth; a player's strike ends the season

after just 117 games, ending Tony Gwynn's bid to bat .400 and preserving Roger Maris's home run record, which appeared within reach of several players; the Dodgers sign Korean pitching star Chan Ho Park.

1995 Cal Ripken, Jr., breaks Lou Gehrig's record for consecutive games played; Japan's Hideo Nomo becomes a star for the Dodgers, increasing the international appeal of baseball and intensifying major-league scouting activity in Pacific Rim countries.

1996 A barrage of home runs highlights baseball's first full season since 1993, with an unprecedented 43 players hitting 30 or more homers; Baltimore star Roberto Alomar spits in the face of an umpire during an argument, triggering a national debate on the state of baseball and the lack of a commissioner.

1997 Minor-league pitcher Ila Borders becomes the first woman to appear in a regular-season professional baseball game; Japanese pitcher Hideki Irabu commands a $13 million contract with the Yankees—the highest ever for a major-league "rookie." Mark McGwire and Ken Griffey, Jr., make a run at Roger Maris's home-run record but fall short (McGwire finishing with 58 homers and Griffey with 56).

APPENDIX A
Baseball Pennant Winners

Post-Season Championships

National Association

1871	Philadelphia Athletics
1872	Boston Red Stockings
1873	Boston Red Stockings
1874	Boston Red Stockings
1875	Boston Red Stockings

National League

1876	Chicago White Stockings
1877	Boston Red Caps
1878	Boston Red Caps
1879	Providence Grays
1880	Chicago White Stockings
1881	Chicago White Stockings

		American Association
1882	Chicago White Stockings	Cincinnati Red Stockings
1883	Boston Beaneaters	Philadelphia Athletics

			Union Association	World Series
1884	Providence Grays	New York Metropolitans	St. Louis Maroons	Providence 3; New York 0
1885	Chicago White Stockings	St. Louis Browns		Chicago 3; St. Louis 3 (1 tie)
1886	Chicago White Stockings	St. Louis Browns		St. Louis 4; Chicago 2
1887	Detroit Wolverines	St. Louis Browns		Detroit 10; St. Louis 5
1888	New York Giants	St. Louis Browns		New York 6; St. Louis 4
1889	New York Giants	Brooklyn Bridegrooms		New York 6; Brooklyn 3

			Players League	
1890	Brooklyn Bridegrooms	Louisville Colonels	Boston Reds	Brooklyn 3; Louisville 3 (1 tie)
1891	Boston Beaneaters	Boston Reds		No Competition Held

		Temple Cup*
1892	Boston Beaneaters	Boston 5; Cleveland 0 (1 tie)
1893	Boston Beaneaters	No Competition Held
1894	Baltimore Orioles	New York 4; Baltimore 0
1895	Baltimore Orioles	Cleveland 4; Baltimore 1
1896	Baltimore Orioles	Baltimore 4; Cleveland 0
1897	Boston Beaneaters	Baltimore 4; Boston 1
1898	Boston Beaneaters	No Competition Held
1899	Brooklyn Bridegrooms	No Competition Held

	National League			Chronicle-Telegraph Cup*
1900	Brooklyn Superbas			Brooklyn 3; Pittsburgh 1

		American League		
1901	Pittsburgh Pirates	Chicago White Stockings		
1902	Pittsburgh Pirates	Philadelphia Athletics		

				World Series
1903	Pittsburgh Pirates	Boston Pilgrims		Boston 5; Pittsburgh 3
1904	New York Giants	Boston Pilgrims		No Competition Held
1905	New York Giants	Philadelphia Athletics		New York 4; Philadelphia 1
1906	Chicago Cubs	Chicago White Sox		Chicago (A) 4; Chicago (N) 2
1907	Chicago Cubs	Detroit Tigers		Chicago 4; Detroit 0 (1 tie)
1908	Chicago Cubs	Detroit Tigers		Chicago 4; Detroit 1
1909	Pittsburgh Pirates	Detroit Tigers		Pittsburgh 4; Detroit 3
1910	Chicago Cubs	Philadelphia Athletics		Philadelphia 4; Chicago 1
1911	New York Giants	Philadelphia Athletics		Philadelphia 4; New York 2
1912	New York Giants	Boston Red Sox		Boston 4; New York 3
1913	New York Giants	Philadelphia Athletics		Philadelphia 4; New York 1
			Federal League	
1914	Boston Braves	Philadelphia Athletics	Indianapolis Hoosiers	Boston 4; Philadelphia 0
1915	Philadelphia Phillies	Boston Red Sox	Chicago Whales	Boston 4; Philadelphia 1
1916	Brooklyn Robins	Boston Red Sox		Boston 4; Brooklyn 0
1917	New York Giants	Chicago White Sox		Chicago 4; New York 2
1918	Chicago Cubs	Boston Red Sox		Boston 4; Chicago 2
1919	Cincinnati Reds	Chicago White Sox		Cincinnati 5; Chicago 3
1920	Brooklyn Robins	Cleveland Indians		Cleveland 5; Brooklyn 2
1921	New York Giants	New York Yankees		New York (N) 5; New York (A) 3
1922	New York Giants	New York Yankees		New York (N) 4; New York (A) 0 (1 tie)
1923	New York Giants	New York Yankees		New York (A) 4; New York (N) 2
1924	New York Giants	Washington Senators		Washington 4; New York 3
1925	Pittsburgh Pirates	Washington Senators		Pittsburgh 4; Washington 3
1926	St. Louis Cardinals	New York Yankees		St. Louis 4; New York 3
1927	Pittsburgh Pirates	New York Yankees		New York 4; Pittsburgh 0
1928	St. Louis Cardinals	New York Yankees		New York 4; St. Louis 0
1929	Chicago Cubs	Philadelphia Athletics		Philadelphia 4; Chicago 1
1930	St. Louis Cardinals	Philadelphia Athletics		Philadelphia 4; St. Louis 2
1931	St. Louis Cardinals	Philadelphia Athletics		St. Louis 4; Philadelphia 3
1932	Chicago Cubs	New York Yankees		New York 4; Chicago 0
1933	New York Giants	Washington Senators		New York 4; Washington 1
1934	St. Louis Cardinals	Detroit Tigers		St. Louis 4; Detroit 3
1935	Chicago Cubs	Detroit Tigers		Detroit 4; Chicago 2
1936	New York Giants	New York Yankees		New York (A) 4; New York (N) 2

1937	New York Giants	New York Yankees	New York (A) 4; New York (N) 1
1938	Chicago Cubs	New York Yankees	New York 4; Chicago 0
1939	Cincinnati Reds	New York Yankees	New York 4; Cincinnati 0
1940	Cincinnati Reds	Detroit Tigers	Cincinnati 4; Detroit 3
1941	Brooklyn Dodgers	New York Yankees	New York 4; Brooklyn 1
1942	St. Louis Cardinals	New York Yankees	St. Louis 4; New York 1
1943	St. Louis Cardinals	New York Yankees	New York 4; St. Louis 1
1944	St. Louis Cardinals	St. Louis Browns	St. Louis (N) 4; St. Louis (A) 2
1945	Chicago Cubs	Detroit Tigers	Detroit 4; Chicago 3
1946	St. Louis Cardinals	Boston Red Sox	St. Louis 4; Boston 3
1947	Brooklyn Dodgers	New York Yankees	New York 4; Brooklyn 3
1948	Boston Braves	Cleveland Indians	Cleveland 4; Boston 2
1949	Brooklyn Dodgers	New York Yankees	New York 4; Brooklyn 1
1950	Philadelphia Phillies	New York Yankees	New York 4; Philadelphia 0
1951	New York Giants	New York Yankees	New York (A) 4; New York (N) 2
1952	Brooklyn Dodgers	New York Yankees	New York 4; Brooklyn 3
1953	Brooklyn Dodgers	New York Yankees	New York 4; Brooklyn 2
1954	New York Giants	Cleveland Indians	New York 4; Cleveland 0
1955	Brooklyn Dodgers	New York Yankees	Brooklyn 4; New York 3
1956	Brooklyn Dodgers	New York Yankees	New York 4; Brooklyn 3
1957	Milwaukee Braves	New York Yankees	Milwaukee 4; New York 3
1958	Milwaukee Braves	New York Yankees	New York 4; Milwaukee 3
1959	Los Angeles Dodgers	Chicago White Sox	Los Angeles 4; Chicago 2
1960	Pittsburgh Pirates	New York Yankees	Pittsburgh 4; New York 3
1961	Cincinnati Reds	New York Yankees	New York 4; Cincinnati 1
1962	San Francisco Giants	New York Yankees	New York 4; San Francisco 3
1963	Los Angeles Dodgers	New York Yankees	Los Angeles 4; New York 0
1964	St. Louis Cardinals	New York Yankees	St. Louis 4; New York 3
1965	Los Angeles Dodgers	Minnesota Twins	Los Angeles 4; Minnesota 3
1966	Los Angeles Dodgers	Baltimore Orioles	Baltimore 4; Los Angeles 0
1967	St. Louis Cardinals	Boston Red Sox	St. Louis 4; Boston 3
1968	St. Louis Cardinals	Detroit Tigers	Detroit 4; St. Louis 3
1969	New York Mets	Baltimore Orioles	New York 4; Baltimore 1
1970	Cincinnati Reds	Baltimore Orioles	Baltimore 4; Cincinnati 1
1971	Pittsburgh Pirates	Baltimore Orioles	Pittsburgh 4; Baltimore 3
1972	Cincinnati Reds	Oakland A's	Oakland 4; Cincinnati 3
1973	New York Mets	Oakland A's	Oakland 4; New York 3
1974	Los Angeles Dodgers	Oakland A's	Oakland 4; Los Angeles 2
1975	Cincinnati Reds	Boston Red Sox	Cincinnati 4; Boston 3
1976	Cincinnati Reds	New York Yankees	Cincinnati 4; New York 0
1977	Los Angeles Dodgers	New York Yankees	New York 4; Los Angeles 2
1978	Los Angeles Dodgers	New York Yankees	New York 4; Los Angeles 2
1979	Pittsburgh Pirates	Baltimore Orioles	Pittsburgh 4; Baltimore 3
1980	Philadelphia Phillies	Kansas City Royals	Philadelphia 4; Kansas City 2
1981	Los Angeles Dodgers	New York Yankees	Los Angeles 4; New York 2

1982	St. Louis Cardinals	Milwaukee Brewers	St. Louis 4; Milwaukee 3
1983	Philadelphia Phillies	Baltimore Orioles	Baltimore 4; Philadelphia 1
1984	San Diego Padres	Detroit Tigers	Detroit 4; San Diego 1
1985	St. Louis Cardinals	Kansas City Royals	St. Louis 4; Kansas City 3
1986	New York Mets	Boston Red Sox	New York 4; Boston 3
1987	St. Louis Cardinals	Minnesota Twins	Minnesota 4; St. Louis 3
1988	Los Angeles Dodgers	Oakland A's	Los Angeles 4; Oakland 1
1989	San Francisco Giants	Oakland A's	Oakland 4; San Francisco 0
1990	Cincinnati Reds	Oakland A's	Cincinnati 4; Oakland 0
1991	Atlanta Braves	Minnesota Twins	Minnesota 4; Atlanta 3
1992	Atlanta Braves	Toronto Blue Jays	Toronto 4; Atlanta 2
1993	Philadelphia Phillies	Toronto Blue Jays	Toronto 4; Philadelphia 2
1994	Strike—No Pennant Winners Declared		No Competition Held
1995	Atlanta Braves	Cleveland Indians	Atlanta 4; Cleveland 2
1996	Atlanta Braves	New York Yankees	New York 4; Atlanta 2
1997	Florida Marlins	Cleveland Indians	Florida 4; Cleveland 3

APPENDIX B
Baseball's All-Time Leaders

The following pages contain the all-time leaders in 16 key statistical catagories, listing the Top 10 in each over a single season and over an entire career. The statistics cover the period from 1876 to 1997 and make no differentiation between players in the 19th and 20th centuries. Each list is accompanied by a brief explanation of what it took to break into the Top 10.

Hits—Season
Every player on the list was a line-drive specialist playing in a cozy ballpark during a particularly good hitter's year. The most impressive single-season total in recent years was Joe Torre's 230 hits for the Cardinals in 1971—good for only 32nd on the all-time list.

Player	Team	Year	Hits
George Sisler	St. Louis Browns	1920	257
Lefty O'Doul	Philadelphia Phillies	1929	254
Bill Terry	New York Giants	1930	254
Al Simmons	Philadelphia Athletics	1925	253
Rogers Hornsby	St. Louis Cardinals	1922	250
Chuck Klein	Philadelphia Phillies	1930	250
Ty Cobb	Detroit Tigers	1911	248
George Sisler	St. Louis Browns	1922	246
Heinie Manush	St. Louis Browns	1928	241
Babe Herman	Brooklyn Dodgers	1930	241

Hits—Career
Of the all-time Top 10 in hits, only two—Rose and Collins—were "singles" hitters. The other eight were among the supreme power hitters of their respective eras. [Note: Eddie Murray, still active in 1997, is now in the top 10.]

Player	Years	Hits
Pete Rose	1963–86	4256
Ty Cobb	1905-28	4189
Hank Aaron	1954–76	3771
Stan Musial	1941–63	3630
Tris Speaker	1907–28	3514
Carl Yastrzemski	1960–83	3419
Honus Wagner	1897–17	3415
Eddie Collins	1906–30	3315
Willie Mays	1951–73	3283
Eddie Murray	1977–97	3255

Runs—Season

Aside from the marvelous seasons turned in by 20th century stars Babe Ruth and Lou Gehrig, every major run-scoring mark was set by players who performed from the late 1880s to the mid-1890s. During this period, pitchers were adjusting to new restrictions that were designed to boost baseball's offensive production.

Player	Team	Year	Runs
Billy Hamilton	Philadelphia Phillies	1894	192
Tom Brown	Boston Reds	1891	177
Babe Ruth	New York Yankees	1921	177
Tip O'Neill	St. Louis Browns	1887	167
Lou Gehrig	New York Yankees	1936	167
Billy Hamilton	Philadelphia Phillies	1895	166
Willie Keeler	Baltimore Orioles	1894	165
Joe Kelley	Baltimore Orioles	1894	165
Arlie Latham	St. Louis Browns	1887	163
Babe Ruth	New York Yankees	1928	163
Lou Gehrig	New York Yankees	1931	163

Runs—Career

The players on this list prove that, over the long haul, scoring runs is more a matter of great hitting than great base running.

Player	Years	Runs
Ty Cobb	1905–28	2246
Hank Aaron	1954–76	2174
Babe Ruth	1914–35	2174
Pete Rose	1963–86	2165
Willie Mays	1951–73	2062
Stan Musial	1941–63	1949
Rickey Henderson	1979–97	1913
Lou Gehrig	1923–39	1888
Tris Speaker	1907–28	1882
Mel Ott	1926–47	1859

Home Runs—Season

With the further thinning of major-league pitching through expansion, some experts believe that half the names on this list will change over the next few years.

Player	Team	Year	Home Runs
Roger Maris	New York Yankees	1961	61
Babe Ruth	New York Yankees	1927	60
Babe Ruth	New York Yankees	1921	59
Jimmie Foxx	Philadelphia Athletics	1932	58
Hank Greenberg	Detroit Tigers	1938	58
Mark McGwire	A's, Cardinals	1997	58
Hack Wilson	Chicago Cubs	1930	56
Ken Griffey, Jr.	Seattle Mariners	1997	56
Babe Ruth	New York Yankees	1920	54
Babe Ruth	New York Yankees	1928	54

Home Runs—Career

There is no cheap way to make it into the all-time Top 10 in home runs. These players earned it one round-tripper at a time.

Player	Years	Home Runs
Hank Aaron	1954–76	755
Babe Ruth	1914–35	714
Willie Mays	1951–73	660
Frank Robinson	1956–76	586
Harmon Killebrew	1954–75	573
Reggie Jackson	1967–87	563
Mike Schmidt	1972–89	548
Mickey Mantle	1951–68	536
Jimmie Foxx	1925–45	534
Willie McCovey	1959–80	521
Ted Williams	1939–60	521

Home Run Frequency—Season

This statistic measures the percentage of official at bats that result in home runs. It is perhaps the best way to measure how lethal a hitter can be whenever he walks to the plate. These players all had monster seasons.

Player	Team	Year	HR Pct.
Mark McGwire	Oakland A's	1996	12.3
Babe Ruth	New York Yankees	1920	11.8
Babe Ruth	New York Yankees	1927	11.1
Babe Ruth	New York Yankees	1921	10.9
Mark McGwire	A's, Cardinals	1997	10.7
Mickey Mantle	New York Yankees	1961	10.5
Hank Greenberg	Detroit Tigers	1938	10.4
Roger Maris	New York Yankees	1961	10.3
Babe Ruth	New York Yankees	1928	10.1
Jimmie Foxx	Philadelphia Athletics	1932	9.9

Home Run Frequency—Career

This list is similar to the all-time home run list, with two exceptions. First, it recognizes the achievements of Kiner and Kingman, whose careers ended somewhat abruptly. Second, it includes active players who have yet to experience the declining years in their careers.

Player	Years	HR Pct.
Babe Ruth	1914–35	8.5
Mark McGwire	1986–97	8.4
Ralph Kiner	1946–55	7.1
Harmon Killebrew	1954–75	7.0
Ted Williams	1939–60	6.7
Dave Kingman	1971–86	6.6
Mickey Mantle	1951–68	6.6
Jimmie Foxx	1925–45	6.6
Mike Schmidt	1972–89	6.6
Jose Canseco	1985–97	6.4

Runs Batted In—Season

This list illustrates that it takes a great hitter to be a great RBI man. But a closer look at the teams and years represented also reveals that you need some great hitters to get on base in front of you. Indeed, each of these players had a couple of top "table-setters" batting in front of him.

Player	Team	Year	RBIs
Hack Wilson	Chicago Cubs	1930	190
Lou Gehrig	New York Yankees	1931	184
Hank Greenberg	Detroit Tigers	1937	183
Lou Gehrig	New York Yankees	1927	175
Jimmie Foxx	Boston Red Sox	1938	175
Lou Gehrig	New York Yankees	1930	174
Babe Ruth	New York Yankees	1921	171
Chuck Klein	Philadelphia Phillies	1930	170
Hank Greenberg	Detroit Tigers	1935	170
Jimmie Foxx	Philadelphia Athletics	1932	169

Runs Batted In—Career

This is an interesting assortment of players and remarkably similar to the all-time runs scored list.

Player	Years	RBIs
Hank Aaron	1954–76	2297
Babe Ruth	1914–35	2213
Lou Gehrig	1923–39	1995
Stan Musial	1941–63	1951
Ty Cobb	1905–28	1937
Jimmie Foxx	1925–45	1922
Eddie Murray	1977–97	1917
Willie Mays	1951–73	1903

| Cap Anson | 1876–1897 | 1879 |
| Mel Ott | 1926–47 | 1860 |

Batting Average—Season

Seven of the following 10 players posted their astronomical batting averages during seasons when averages in general were extremely high. The remaining three—Barnes, Dunlap, and Lajoie—were established stars joining brand new leagues, where the quality of pitching was highly suspect. The most impressive mark may belong to Hornsby, who topped the 1924 runner-up by 49 points.

Player	Team	Year	BA	Points Ahead
Hugh Duffy	Boston Beaneaters	1894	.440	24
Tip O'Neill	St. Louis Browns	1887	.435	33
Ross Barnes	Chicago White Stockings	1876	.429	63
Napoleon Lajoie	Philadelphia Athletics	1901	.426	86
Willie Keeler	Baltimore Orioles	1897	.424	34
Rogers Hornsby	St. Louis Cardinals	1924	.424	49
George Sisler	St. Louis Browns	1922	.420	19
Ty Cobb	Detroit Tigers	1911	.420	12
Fred Dunlap	St. Louis Maroons	1884	.412	52
Ed Delahanty	Philadelphia Phillies	1899	.410	14

Batting Average—Career

A lot of players have spent time among the all-time Top 10 batters, but because the declining years of a player's career typically drag down his lifetime average, few have had what it takes to stay. Jackson, Delahanty, Hamilton, and Heilmann each experienced an abrupt end to his career, which helped them remain on the list.

Player	Years	BA
Ty Cobb	1905–28	.366
Rogers Hornsby	1915–37	.358
Joe Jackson	1908–20	.356
Ed Delahanty	1888–03	.346
Tris Speaker	1907–28	.345
Ted Williams	1939–60	.344
Billy Hamilton	1888–01	.344
Dan Brouthers	1879–04	.342
Babe Ruth	1914–35	.342
Harry Heilmann	1914–32	.342

Slugging Average—Season

This statistic measures the number of total bases per official at bat. It is similar to batting average but gives a hitter additional credit for extra base hits. If a single category best reflects how good a hitter Babe Ruth was, this would be the one. The only recent player on the list, Jeff Bagwell, was on a hot streak when his hand was broken by a pitch, and therefore he never had the chance to "cool off."

Player	Team	Year	SA
Babe Ruth	New York Yankees	1920	.847
Babe Ruth	New York Yankees	1921	.846

Babe Ruth	New York Yankees	1927	.772
Lou Gehrig	New York Yankees	1927	.765
Babe Ruth	New York Yankees	1923	.764
Rogers Hornsby	St. Louis Cardinals	1925	.756
Jeff Bagwell	Houston Astros	1994	.750
Jimmie Foxx	Philadelphia Athletics	1932	.749
Babe Ruth	New York Yankees	1924	.739
Babe Ruth	New York Yankees	1926	.737

Slugging Average—Career

The retired players on this list were great in their prime years but distinguished themselves from other power hitters because their production did not drop off dramatically during the latter stages of their careers.

Player	Years	SA
Babe Ruth	1914–35	.690
Ted Williams	1939–60	.634
Lou Gehrig	1923–39	.632
Jimmie Foxx	1925–45	.609
Hank Greenberg	1930–47	.605
Frank Thomas	1990–97	.600
Joe DiMaggio	1936–51	.579
Rogers Hornsby	1915–37	.577
Albert Belle	1989–97	.566
Ken Griffey, Jr.	1989–97	.564

Stolen Bases—Season

The dramatic restrictions placed upon pitchers in 1887 kept them from faking out baserunners, and several players took advantage of this situation to rack up huge stolen base totals. It took pitchers about five years before they learned how to hold runners on.

Player	Team	Year	SB
Hugh Nicol	Cincinnati Reds	1887	138
Rickey Henderson	Oakland A's	1982	130
Arlie Latham	St. Louis Browns	1887	129
Lou Brock	St. Louis Cardinals	1974	118
Charlie Comiskey	St. Louis Browns	1887	117
John Ward	New York Giants	1887	111
Billy Hamilton	Kansas City Cowboys	1889	111
Billy Hamilton	Philadelphia Phillies	1891	111
Vince Coleman	St. Louis Cardinals	1985	110
Arlie Latham	St. Louis Browns	1888	109
Vince Coleman	St. Louis Cardinals	1987	109

Stolen Bases—Career

Though all of these players rank among the all-time greats, they are not necessarily the fastest or most talented base runners in history. What they have in common was that they played when the stolen base was a popular offensive weapon, and they did not lose their speed in their 30's, as their other talents began to decline.

Player	Years	SB
Rickey Henderson	1979–97	1231
Lou Brock	1961–79	938
Billy Hamilton	1888–01	912
Ty Cobb	1905–28	892
Tim Raines	1979–97	795
Vince Coleman	1985–1996	752
Eddie Collins	1906–30	744
Arlie Latham	1880–09	739
Max Carey	1910–29	738
Honus Wagner	1897–17	722

Pitching Victories—Season

Each person on this list pitched during the 1870s and 1880s, when a top starter was expected to win 30 to 40 games. All but two played when pitchers were allowed to take running starts before delivering the ball to the plate. During the past century, only two men have won as many as 40 games in a season, and only four have won 30 or more since the end of the Dead Ball era.

Player	Team	Year	Wins
Old Hoss Radbourn	Providence Grays	1884	59
John Clarkson	Chicago White Stockings	1885	53
Guy Hecker	Louisville Eclipse	1884	52
John Clarkson	Boston Beaneaters	1889	49
Old Hoss Radbourn	Providence Grays	1883	48
Charlie Buffington	Boston Beaneaters	1884	48
Al Spalding	Chicago White Stockings	1876	47
John Ward	Providence Grays	1879	47
Pud Galvin	Buffalo Bisons	1883	46
Pud Galvin	Buffalo Bisons	1884	46
Matt Kilroy	Baltimore Orioles	1887	46

Pitching Victories—Career

The players on this list fit neatly into two categories, although they have one thing in common: they pitched at a very high level for a far longer period than their contemporaries. The 19th century hurlers played at a time when a team's top starter might go to the mound 50 to 70 times a season, and therefore win 30 to 40 games a year. The 20th century pitchers racked up fewer wins per season because they were members of three- and four-man rotations, but they pitched for many more years.

Player	Years	Wins
Cy Young	1890–11	511
Walter Johnson	1907–27	417

Grover Alexander	1911–30	373
Christy Mathewson	1900–16	373
Warren Spahn	1942–65	363
Kid Nichols	1890–06	361
Pud Galvin	1879–92	360
Tim Keefe	1880–93	342
Steve Carlton	1965–88	329
John Clarkson	1882–94	328

Winning Percentage—Season

This statistic, which measures the percentage of a pitcher's decisions that are victories, is as much a function of not losing as it is of winning. It is interesting to note that none of the pitchers on the Top 10 list for wins in a season make this list.

Player	Team	Year	Pct.
Roy Face	Pittsburgh Pirates	1959	.947
Greg Maddux	Atlanta Braves	1995	.905
Randy Johnson	Seattle Mariners	1995	.900
Ron Guidry	New York Yankees	1978	.893
Freddie Fitzsimmons	Brooklyn Dodgers	1940	.889
Lefty Grove	Philadelphia Athletics	1931	.886
Preacher Roe	Brooklyn Dodgers	1951	.880
Fred Goldsmith	Chicago White Stockings	1880	.875
Joe Wood	Boston Red Sox	1912	.872
David Cone	New York Mets	1988	.870

Winning Percentage—Career

There is a little luck involved in making this list, although each of the following pitchers ranked among the toughest of his day. Because they all played for very good teams during their prime years, they rarely lost a well-pitched game and often won when they did not have their best stuff. Caruthers and Foutz, for instance, pitched their prime years for the dominant St. Louis Browns of the late 1880s and finished their careers together with the talented Brooklyn Bridegroom clubs in the early 1890s.

Player	Years	Pct.
Dave Foutz	1884–94	.690
Whitey Ford	1950–67	.690
Bob Caruthers	1884–92	.688
Lefty Grove	1925–41	.680
Vic Raschi	1945–55	.667
Larry Corcoran	1880–87	.665
Christy Mathewson	1900–16	.665
Sam Leever	1898–10	.660
Sal Maglie	1945–58	.657
Sandy Koufax	1955–66	.655

Strikeouts—Season

A look at the seasons during which 8 of the 10 players on this list amassed their great strikeout totals makes it easy to understand why the rules governing pitchers began to change dramatically in 1887. They were not "flame throwers," they had just learned how to baffle hitters from 50 feet away. In fact, of the 19th century pitchers listed here, only Hugh Daily—who, like Jim Abbott, only had one hand—was a strikeout pitcher in the modern sense.

Player	Team	Year	Ks
Matt Kilroy	Baltimore Orioles	1886	513
Toad Ramsey	Louisville Colonels	1886	499
Hugh Daily	Chicago/Pittsburgh Unions and Washington Nationals	1884	483
Dupee Shaw	Detroit Wolverines and Boston Reds	1884	451
Old Hoss Radbourn	Providence Grays	1884	441
Charlie Buffington	Boston Beaneaters	1884	417
Guy Hecker	Louisville Eclipse	1884	385
Nolan Ryan	California Angels	1973	383
Sandy Koufax	Los Angeles Dodgers	1965	382
Bill Sweeney	Baltimore Unions	1884	374

Strikeouts—Career

An interesting list, in that it includes only four pitchers—Ryan, Seaver, Johnson, and Gibson—whose strikeout pitch was a fastball. The others used sinkers, sliders, knuckleballs, curves, and an occasional spitter.

Player	Years	Ks
Nolan Ryan	1966–93	5714
Steve Carlton	1965–88	4136
Bert Blyleven	1970–92	3701
Tom Seaver	1967–86	3640
Don Sutton	1966–88	3574
Gaylord Perry	1962–83	3534
Walter Johnson	1907–27	3509
Phil Niekro	1964–87	3342
Fergie Jenkins	1965–83	3192
Bob Gibson	1959–75	3117

ERA—Season

Remarkable years by remarkable pitchers, but all were turned in during seasons when pitchers dominated hitters.

Player	Team	Year	ERA
Tim Keefe	Troy Trojans	1880	0.86
Dutch Leonard	Boston Red Sox	1914	0.96
Mordecai Brown	Chicago Cubs	1906	1.04
Bob Gibson	St. Louis Cardinals	1968	1.12
Christy Mathewson	New York Giants	1909	1.14
Walter Johnson	Washington Senators	1913	1.14
Jack Pfiester	Chicago Cubs	1907	1.15
Addie Joss	Cleveland Naps	1908	1.16

Carl Lundgren	Chicago Cubs	1907	1.17
Denny Driscoll	Pittsburgh Alleghenys	1882	1.21

ERA—Career

Every hurler on this list pitched during a time when pitchers dominated hitters, although Johnson played for several years during the high-scoring 1920s.

Player	Years	ERA
Ed Walsh	1904–17	1.82
Addie Joss	1902–10	1.89
Mordecai Brown	1903–16	2.06
John Ward	1878–84	2.10
Christy Mathewson	1900–16	2.13
Rube Waddell	1897–10	2.16
Walter Johnson	1907–27	2.17
Orval Overall	1905–13	2.23
Tommy Bond	1876–84	2.25
Ed Reulbach	1905–17	2.28
Will White	1877–86	2.28

Innings Pitched—Season

This list is little more than a tribute to the workhorse pitchers of the 19th century, for not a single 20th century hurler even makes the Top 100 in this category.

Player	Team	Year	IP
Will White	Cincinnati Reds	1879	680
Old Hoss Radbourn	Providence Grays	1884	678 2/3
Guy Hecker	Louisville Eclipse	1884	670 2/3
Jim McCormick	Cleveland Blues	1880	657 2/3
Pud Galvin	Buffalo Bisons	1883	656 1/3
Pud Galvin	Buffalo Bisons	1884	636 1/3
Old Hoss Radbourn	Providence Grays	1883	632 1/3
John Clarkson	Chicago White Stockings	1885	623
Jim Devlin	Louisville Grays	1876	622
Bill Hutchinson	Chicago Colts	1892	622

Innings Pitched—Career

Note that only one player on the above list makes this one. There is nothing like a couple of 600-inning seasons to blow out a pitcher's arm.

Player	Years	IP
Cy Young	1890–11	7356
Pud Galvin	1879–92	5941 1/3
Walter Johnson	1907–27	5914 1/3
Phil Niekro	1964–87	5404 1/3
Nolan Ryan	1966–93	5386

Gaylord Perry	1962–83	5350 1/3
Don Sutton	1966–88	5282 1/3
Warren Spahn	1942–65	5243 2/3
Steve Carlton	1965–88	5217 1/3
Grover Alexander	1911–30	5190

Hits Per Game—Season

Imagine having your best stuff just about every time out. For one season, these pitchers did just that.

Player	Team	Year	Hits/9 IP
Nolan Ryan	California Angels	1972	5.3
Luis Tiant	Cleveland Indians	1968	5.3
Nolan Ryan	Texas Rangers	1991	5.3
Ed Reulbach	Chicago Cubs	1906	5.3
Dutch Leonard	Boston Red Sox	1914	5.6
Carl Lundgren	Chicago Cubs	1907	5.7
Sid Fernandez	New York Mets	1985	5.7
Tommy Byrne	New York Yankees	1949	5.7
Dave McNally	Baltimore Orioles	1968	5.8
Sandy Koufax	Los Angeles Dodgers	1965	5.8

Hits Per Game—Career

The following pitchers rank as the toughest to hit over the long haul. An interesting mix of old and new, with a few surprises.

Player	Years	Hits/9 IP
Nolan Ryan	1966–93	6.6
Sandy Koufax	1955–66	6.8
Randy Johnson	1988–97	6.9
Sid Fernandez	1983–97	6.9
J.R. Richard	1971–80	6.9
Andy Messersmith	1968–79	6.9
Hoyt Wilhelm	1952–72	7.0
Sam McDowell	1961–75	7.0
Ed Walsh	1904–17	7.1
Bob Turley	1951–63	7.2

Strikeouts Per Game—Season

The players on this list are the ones one would expect to find. The dates illustrate just how undisciplined hitters have become over the past three decades.

Player	Team	Year	SO/9 IP
Randy Johnson	Seattle Mariners	1995	12.4
Randy Johnson	Seattle Mariners	1997	12.3
Nolan Ryan	Houston Astros	1987	11.5
Dwight Gooden	New York Mets	1984	11.4

Pedro Martinez	Montreal Expos	1997	11.4
Curt Schilling	Philadelphia Phillies	1997	11.3
Nolan Ryan	Texas Rangers	1989	11.3
Hideo Nomo	Los Angeles Dodgers	1995	11.1
Randy Johnson	Seattle Mariners	1993	10.9
Sam McDowell	Cleveland Indians	1965	10.7

Strikeouts Per Game—Career

Player	Years	SO/9 IP
Randy Johnson	1988–97	10.4
Nolan Ryan	1966–93	9.6
Sandy Koufax	1955–66	9.3
Sam McDowell	1961–75	8.9
Roger Clemens	1984–97	8.5
Sid Fernandez	1983–97	8.4
J.R. Richard	1971–80	8.4
David Cone	1986–97	8.4
Bob Veale	1962–74	8.0
Jose Rijo	1984–96	7.8

Saves—Season

Single-season save totals are a combination of great pressure pitching and enough chances to close out tight ballgames. The following players did plenty of both.

Player	Team	Year	Saves
Bobby Thigpen	Chicago White Sox	1990	57
Randy Myers	Chicago Cubs	1993	53
Dennis Eckersley	Oakland A's	1992	51
Dennis Eckersley	Oakland A's	1990	48
Rod Beck	San Francisco Giants	1993	48
Lee Smith	St. Louis Cardinals	1991	47
Lee Smith	St. Louis Cardinals	1993	46
Dave Righetti	New York Yankees	1986	46
Bryan Harvey	California Angels	1991	46
Jose Mesa	Cleveland Indians	1995	46

Saves—Career

The closer's job is one of the toughest in baseball to keep. Unlike a starting pitcher or a position player, a reliever is rarely allowed to go more than five or six games without being replaced.

Player	Years	Saves
Lee Smith	1980–97	478
Dennis Eckersley	1975–97	389
Jeff Reardon	1979–94	367

John Franco	1984–97	359
Rollie Fingers	1968–85	341
Randy Myers	1985–97	319
Tom Henke	1982–95	311
Rich Gossage	1972–94	310
Bruce Sutter	1976–88	300
Doug Jones	1982–97	278

APPENDIX C
Post-Season Awards

Year	NL MVP	AL MVP
1911[1]	Fred Schulte, Cubs *3B*	Ty Cobb, Tigers *CF*
1912	Larry Doyle, Giants *2B*	Tris Speaker, Red Sox *CF*
1913	Jake Daubert, Robins *1B*	Walter Johnson, Senators *P*
1914	Johnny Evers, Braves *2B*	Eddie Collins, Athletics *2B*
1922[2]		George Sisler, Browns *1B*
1923		Babe Ruth, Yankees *RF*
1924	Dazzy Vance, Robins *P*	Walter Johnson, Senators *P*
1925	Rogers Hornsby, Cardinals *2B*	Roger Peckinpaugh, Senators *SS*
1926	Bob O'Farrell, Cardinals *C*	George Burns, Indians *1B*
1927	Paul Waner, Pirates *RF*	Lou Gehrig, Yankees *1B*
1928	Jim Bottomley, Cardinals *1B*	Mickey Cochrane, Athletics *C*
1929	Rogers Hornsby, Cubs *2B*	
1931[3]	Frankie Frisch, Cardinals *2B*	Lefty Grove, Athletics *P*
1932	Chuck Klein, Phillies *RF*	Jimmie Foxx, Athletics *1B*
1933	Carl Hubbell, Giants *P*	Jimmie Foxx, Athletics *1B*
1934	Dizzy Dean, Cardinals *P*	Mickey Cochrane, Tigers *C*
1935	Gabby Hartnett, Cubs *C*	Hank Greenberg, Tigers *1B*
1936	Carl Hubbell, Giants *P*	Lou Gehrig, Yankees *1B*
1937	Joe Medwick, Cardinals *LF*	Charlie Gehringer, Tigers *2B*
1938	Ernie Lombardi, Reds *C*	Jimmie Foxx, Red Sox *1B*
1939	Bucky Walters, Reds *P*	Joe DiMaggio, Yankees *CF*
1940	Moose McCormick, Reds *1B*	Hank Greenberg, Tigers *LF*
1941	Dolph Camilli, Dodgers *1B*	Joe DiMaggio, Yankees *CF*
1942	Mort Cooper, Cardinals *P*	Joe Gordon, Yankees *2B*
1943	Stan Musial, Cardinals *RF*	Spud Chandler, Yankees *P*
1944	Marty Marion, Cardinals *SS*	Hal Newhouser, Tigers *P*

1945	Phil Cavaretta, Cubs *1B*	Hal Newhouser, Tigers *P*	
1946	Stan Musial, Cardinals *1B*	Ted Williams, Red Sox *LF*	
1947	Bob Elliott, Braves *3B*	Joe DiMaggio, Yankees *CF*	
1948	Stan Musial, Cardinals *LF*	Lou Boudreau, Indians *SS*	
1949	Jackie Robinson, Dodgers *2B*	Ted Williams, Red Sox *LF*	
1950	Jim Konstanty, Phillies *RP*	Phil Rizzuto, Yankees *SS*	
1951	Roy Campanella, Dodgers *C*	Yogi Berra, Yankees *C*	
1952	Hank Sauer, Cubs *LF*	Bobby Shantz, Athletics *P*	
1953	Roy Campanella, Dodgers *C*	Al Rosen, Indians *3B*	
1954	Willie Mays, Giants *CF*	Yogi Berra, Yankees *C*	
1955	Roy Campanella, Dodgers *C*	Yogi Berra, Yankees *C*	

	NL MVP	**AL MVP**	**NL Cy Young**[4]	**AL Cy Young**
1956	Don Newcombe, Dodgers *P*	Mickey Mantle, Yankees *CF*	Don Newcombe, Dodgers	
1957	Hank Aaron, Braves *RF*	Mickey Mantle, Yankees *CF*	Warren Spahn, Braves	
1958	Ernie Banks, Cubs *SS*	Jackie Jensen, Red Sox *RF*	Bob Turley, Yankees	
1959	Ernie Banks, Cubs *SS*	Nellie Fox, White Sox *2B*		Early Wynn, White Sox
1960	Dick Groat, Pirates *SS*	Roger Maris, Yankees *RF*	Vernon Law, Pirates	
1961	Frank Robinson, Reds *RF*	Roger Maris, Yankees *RF*		Whitey Ford, Yankees
1962	Maury Wills, Dodgers *SS*	Mickey Mantle, Yankees *CF*	Don Drysdale, Dodgers	
1963	Sandy Koufax, Dodgers *P*	Elston Howard, Yankees *C*	Sandy Koufax, Dodgers	
1964	Ken Boyer, Cardinals *3B*	Brooks Robinson, Orioles *3B*		Dean Chance, Angels
1965	Willie Mays, Giants *CF*	Zoilo Versalles, Twins *SS*	Sandy Koufax, Dodgers	
1966	Roberto Clemente, Pirates *RF*	Frank Robinson, Orioles *RF*	Sandy Koufax, Dodgers	
1967	Orlando Cepeda, Cardinals *1B*	Carl Yazstremski, Red Sox *LF*	Mike McCormick, Giants	Jim Lonborg, Red Sox
1968	Bob Gibson, Cardinals *P*	Denny McLain, Tigers *P*	Bob Gibson, Cardinals	Denny McLain, Tigers
1969	Willie McCovey, Giants *1B*	Harmon Killebrew, Twins *3B*	Tom Seaver, Mets	Mike Cuellar, Orioles
1970	Johnny Bench, Reds *C*	Boog Powell, Orioles *1B*	Bob Gibson, Cardinals	Jim Perry, Twins
1971	Joe Torre, Cardinals *3B*	Vida Blue, A's *P*	Fergie Jenkins, Cubs	Vida Blue, A's
1972	Johnny Bench, Reds *C*	Dick Allen, White Sox *1B*	Steve Carlton, Phillies	Gaylord Perry, Indians
1973	Pete Rose, Reds *LF*	Reggie Jackson, A's *RF*	Tom Seaver, Mets	Jim Palmer, Orioles
1974	Steve Garvey, Dodgers *1B*	Jeff Burroughs, Rangers *RF*	Mike Marshall, Dodgers	Catfish Hunter, A's
1975	Joe Morgan, Reds *2B*	Fred Lynn, Red Sox *CF*	Tom Seaver, Mets	Jim Palmer, Orioles
1976	Joe Morgan, Reds *2B*	Thurman Munson, Yankees *C*	Randy Jones, Padres	Jim Palmer, Orioles
1977	George Foster, Reds *LF*	Rod Carew, Twins *1B*	Steve Carlton, Phillies	Sparky Lyle, Yankees
1978	Dave Parker, Pirates *RF*	Jim Rice, Red Sox *LF*	Gaylord Perry, Padres	Ron Guidry, Yankees

1979	Willie Stargell, Pirates *1B* Keith Hernandez, Cardinals *1B*	Don Baylor, Angels *LF*	Bruce Sutter, Cubs	Mike Flanagan, Orioles
1980	Mike Schmidt, Phillies *3B*	George Brett, Royals *3B*	Steve Carlton, Phillies	Steve Stone, Orioles
1981	Mike Schmidt, Phillies *3B*	Rollie Fingers, Brewers *RP*	Fernando Valenzuela, Dodgers	Rollie Fingers, Brewers
1982	Dale Murphy, Braves *CF*	Robin Yount, Brewers *SS*	Steve Carlton, Phillies	Pete Vukovich, Brewers
1983	Dale Murphy, Braves *CF*	Cal Ripken, Jr., Orioles *SS*	John Denny, Phillies	Lamarr Hoyt, White Sox
1984	Ryne Sandberg, Cubs *2B*	Willie Hernandez, Tigers *RP*	Rick Sutcliffe, Cubs	Willie Hernandez, Tigers
1985	Willie McGee, Cardinals *CF*	Don Mattingly, Yankees *1B*	Dwight Gooden, Mets	Bret Saberhagen, Royals
1986	Mike Schmidt, Phillies *3B*	Roger Clemens, Red Sox *P*	Mike Scott, Astros	Roger Clemens, Red Sox
1987	Andre Dawson, Cubs *RF*	George Bell, Blue Jays *LF*	Steve Bedrosian, Phillies	Roger Clemens, Red Sox
1988	Kirk Gibson, Dodgers *LF*	Jose Canseco, A's *RF*	Orel Hershiser, Dodgers	Frank Viola, Twins
1989	Kevin Mitchell, Giants *LF*	Robin Yount, Brewers *CF*	Mark Davis, Padres	Bret Saberhagen, Royals
1990	Barry Bonds, Pirates *LF*	Rickey Henderson, A's *LF*	Doug Drabek, Pirates	Bob Welch, A's
1991	Terry Pendelton, Braves *3B*	Cal Ripken, Jr., Orioles *SS*	Tom Glavine, Braves	Roger Clemens, Red Sox
1992	Barry Bonds, Pirates *LF*	Dennis Eckersley, A's *RP*	Greg Maddux, Cubs	Dennis Eckersley, A's
1993	Barry Bonds, Giants *LF*	Frank Thomas, White Sox *1B*	Greg Maddux, Braves	Jack McDowell, White Sox
1994	Jeff Bagwell, Astros *1B*	Frank Thomas, White Sox *1B*	Greg Maddux, Braves	David Cone, Royals
1995	Barry Larkin, Reds *SS*	Mo Vaughn, Red Sox *1B*	Greg Maddux, Braves	Randy Johnson, Mariners
1996	Ken Caminiti, Padres *3B*	Juan Gonzales, Rangers *RF*	John Smoltz, Braves	Pat Hentgen, Blue Jays

1. 1911–14 Chalmers Award, determined by vote of baseball writers

2. 1922–29 League Award, determined by vote of baseball writers; no NL winner in 1922 & 23, no AL winner in 1929

3. 1931–present Most Valuable Player Award, determined by vote of baseball writers

4. 1956–present, Cy Young Memorial Award determined by vote of baseball writers; only one winner from 1956–66

APPENDIX D

Members of the National Baseball Hall of Fame

Pitchers

Grover Alexander
Chief Bender
Mordecai Brown
Jim Bunning
Steve Carlton
Jack Chesbro
John Clarkson

Stan Coveleski
Dizzy Dean
Don Drysdale
Red Faber
Bob Feller
Rollie Fingers
Whitey Ford
Pud Galvin

Bob Gibson
Lefty Gomez
Burleigh Grimes
Lefty Grove
Jesse Haines
Waite Hoyt
Carl Hubbell
Catfish Hunter

Fergie Jenkins
Walter Johnson
Addie Joss
Tim Keefe
Sandy Koufax
Ted Lyons
Juan Marichal
Rube Marquard

Christy Mathewson
Joe McGinnity
Hal Newhouser
Kid Nichols
Phil Niekro
Jim Palmer
Herb Pennock
Gaylord Perry
Eddie Plank
Old Hoss Radbourn
Eppa Rixey
Robin Roberts
Red Ruffing
Amos Rusie
Tom Seaver
Warren Spahn
Dazzy Vance
Rube Waddell
Ed Walsh
Mickey Welch
Hoyt Wilhelm
Vic Willis
Early Wynn
Cy Young

Catchers

Johnny Bench
Yogi Berra
Roger Bresnahan
Roy Campanella
Mickey Cochrane
Bill Dickey
Buck Ewing
Rick Ferrell
Gabby Hartnett
Ernie Lombardi
Ray Schalk

Infielders

Cap Anson
Luis Aparicio
Luke Appling
Frank Baker
Dave Bancroft

Ernie Banks
Jake Beckley
Jim Bottomley
Lou Boudreau
Dan Brouthers
Rod Carew
Frank Chance
Eddie Collins
Jimmy Collins
Roger Connor
Joe Cronin
Bobby Doerr
Johnny Evers
Nellie Fox
Jimmie Foxx
Frankie Frisch
Lou Gehrig
Charlie Gehringer
Hank Greenberg
Billy Herman
Rogers Hornsby
Travis Jackson
Hugh Jennings
George Kell
George Kelly
Harmon Killebrew
Napoleon Lajoie
Tony Lazzeri
Fred Lindstrom
Rabbit Maranville
Eddie Mathews
Willie McCovey
Johnny Mize
Joe Morgan
Pee Wee Reese
Phil Rizzuto
Brooks Robinson
Jackie Robinson
Mike Schmidt
Red Schoendienst
Joe Sewell
George Sisler
Bill Terry
Joe Tinker

Pie Traynor
Arky Vaughan
Honus Wagner
Bobby Wallace
John Ward

Outfielders

Hank Aaron
Richie Ashburn
Earl Averill
Lou Brock
Jesse Burkett
Max Carey
Fred Clarke
Roberto Clemente
Ty Cobb
Earle Combs
Sam Crawford
Kiki Cuyler
Ed Delahanty
Joe DiMaggio
Hugh Duffy
Elmer Flick
Goose Goslin
Chick Hafey
Billy Hamilton
Harry Heilmann
Harry Hooper
Al Kaline
Willie Keeler
Joe Kelley
King Kelly
Ralph Kiner
Chuck Klein
Mickey Mantle
Heinie Manush
Willie Mays
Tommy McCarthy
Joe Medwick
Stan Musial
Jim O'Rourke
Mel Ott
Sam Rice
Frank Robinson

Edd Roush
Babe Ruth
Al Simmons
Enos Slaughter
Duke Snider
Tris Speaker
Willie Stargell
Sam Thompson
Lloyd Waner
Paul Waner
Zack Wheat
Billy Williams
Ted Williams
Hack Wilson
Carl Yastrzemski
Ross Youngs

Negro Leaguers

Cool Papa Bell
Oscar Charleston
Ray Dandridge
Leon Day
Martin Dihigo
Rube Foster
Willie Foster
Josh Gibson
Monte Irvin
Judy Johnson
Buck Leonard
John Henry Lloyd
Satchel Paige
Willie Wells

Managers

Walter Alston
Leo Durocher
Ned Hanlon
Bucky Harris
Miller Huggins
Tom Lasorda
Al Lopez
Connie Mack
Joe McCarthy
John McGraw

Bill McKechnie
Wilbert Robinson
Casey Stengel
Earl Weaver

Umpires

Al Barlick
Jocko Conlon
Tom Connolly
Billy Evans

Cal Hubbard
Bill Klem
Bill McGowan

Pioneers & Executives

Ed Barrow
Morgan Bulkeley
Alexander Cartwright
Henry Chadwick
Albert Chandler

Charles Comiskey
Candy Cummings
Ford Frick
Warren Giles
Clark Griffith
Will Harridge
William Hulbert
Ban Johnson
Kenesaw Landis
Larry MacPhail

Branch Rickey
Al Spalding
Bill Veeck
George Weiss
George Wright
Harry Wright
Tom Yawkey

For More Information

Books

Burns, Ken, et al. *Twenty-Five Great Moments in Baseball*. New York: Knopf, 1994.

Egan, Terry, et al. *The Macmillan Book of Baseball Stories*. New York: Macmillan, 1994.

Foley, Red. *Red Foley's Best Baseball Book*. New York: Simon & Schuster, 1994.

Ford, Jerry. *The Grand Slam Collection: Have Fun Collecting Baseball Cards*. Minneapolis: Lerner, 1992.

Gutman, Dan. *Baseball's Greatest Games*. New York: Puffin, 1996.

Gutman, Bill. *Baseball*. Tarrytown, NY: Marshall Cavendish, 1990.

Hollander, Zander, ed. *The Baseball Book*. New York: Macmillan, 1991.

Jacobs, William. *They Shaped the Game*. New York: Scribner, 1994.

Silverstein, Herma and Terry J. Dunnahoo. *Baseball Hall of Fame*. Parsippany, NJ: Crestwood House, 1994.

For Advanced Readers

Anderson, Dave. *Pennant Races: Baseball at Its Best*. New York: Doubleday, 1994.

Fiffer, Steve. *How to Watch Baseball*. New York: Facts On File, 1989.

Gilbert, Thomas. *Baseball and the Color Line*. Danbury, CT: Franklin Watts, 1995.

Margolies, Jacob. *The Negro Leagues*. Danbury, CT: Franklin Watts, 1993.

Nemec, David. *The Rules of Baseball*. New York: Burford & Lyons, 1994.

Okent, Daniel and Steve Wuif. *Baseball Anecdotes*. New York: HarperCollins, 1993.

Internet

http://www.majorleaguebaseball.com/
The official web site of Major League Baseball provides team notes, rosters, player information, and more.

http://www.enews.com/bas_hall_fame/
This is the home page of the National Baseball Hall of Fame and Museum.

http://www.totalbaseball.com/homepage.htm
Total Baseball Online is the online home of the *Official Encyclopedia of Major League Baseball*. Read player biographies and team histories; look up player and team statistics; and learn about baseball history!

http://www.ballparks.com
This fun site gives you all the details about major-league ballparks—past, present, and future.

http://www.nc5.infi.net/~moxie/nlb/nlb.html
An exhaustive history of the Negro Leagues, with team histories and player biographies.

http://www.bigleaguers.com/index.html
"The players Choice on the Web," bigleaguers.com provides a personal website for every major-league player.

http://www.sportingnews.com/archives/world-series/
A complete history of the World Series by *The Sporting News*.

http://www.fanlink.com/
Everything you want to know about the minor leagues, including up-to-the-minute scores

Index

Page numbers in *italics* indicate illustrations.

About the Author

Mark Stewart ranks among the busiest sportswriters of the 1990s. He has produced hundreds of profiles on athletes past and present and authored more than 40 books, including biographies of Jeff Gordon, Monica Seles, Steve Young, Hakeem Olajuwan, and Cecil Fielder. A graduate of Duke University, he is currently president of Team Stewart, Inc., a sports information and resource company located in Monmouth County, New Jersey.